KU-425-191

EIGHTH NOTES

VOICES AND FIGURES OF MUSIC AND THE DANCE

EIGHTH NOTES

VOICES AND FIGURES OF MUSIC AND THE DANCE

BY

H. T. PARKER

Essay Index Reprint Series

BOOKS FOR LIBRARIES PRESS
FREEPORT, NEW YORK

First Published 1922
Reprinted 1968

LIBRARY OF CONGRESS CATALOG CARD NUMBER:
68-29236

PRINTED IN THE UNITED STATES OF AMERICA

To

G. S. M.

WHO GAVE ME OPPORTUNITY
AND FREEDOM

EXPLANATION AND ACKNOWLEDGMENT

THIS book is of purpose fragmentary. It does not contain comprehensive and searching "critical studies," but the impressions received and recorded by a reviewer for a newspaper in the daily round of concert-hall, opera house and "copy." At the passing hour in which they were written, at the passing moment in which they may engage the reader, enough if they capture a sensation, decant a mood, reflect a trait, recall achievement, isolate an individualizing quality, hazard an opinion or, best of all, from the tinder of words rekindle the sparks of pleasure remembered. For to give pleasure in kind and degree is essential obligation upon those who are voice to music or body to the dance; while it is incumbent duty upon the reviewer to discern and define (so far as he may) that pleasure.

Outside occasional pages, too few to need specification, these memoranda of the moment were originally strewn through the columns of the *Boston Evening Transcript*. From it, with the permission of the proprietors, they have been astutely assembled and ingeniously coördinated by my friend, Neil Martin. Without his insistence, this book would never have been undertaken; without his persistence, it would never have been accomplished. For such offices of friendship a prefatcry note is polite, prescribed and petty return.

H. T. P.

RANDOLPH,
New Hampshire,
June, 1922.

CONTENTS

I

CONDUCTORS

EIGHTH NOTES

I. Toscanini's Fires

TEUTONIC tradition has died hard in music in America. Once it was preponderant, and it was a primary article of tonal faith that the best music was made only in German-speaking lands and that the best interpreters of it came also from them. The Russians smote the tradition with the hard blows of their symphonies; the new Frenchmen pricked it with the sharp thrusts of their impressions and images; the Italians seared it with the hot fires of their newer work. And every year and almost every week the hearers of music in America, whatever its "school," were becoming a more cosmopolitan public. The tradition that music is a German art—or manufacture—is dead. It is dead, too, with singers and virtuosi of the piano and violin. They come to America and usually receive their deserts, whether Germany happened or not to nurture them and whether Berlin or Munich or Leipzig or Vienna has approved or disapproved them. And this was true, too, for nearly a decade before the war alienated Germany from the rest of the world. With conductors, the German tradition lingered longer and with more reason. In German-speaking opera houses and concert halls conductors were better trained, exercised more authority, excited more public interest, received more public esteem than they did elsewhere.

To Germany, accordingly, the founders of symphony orchestras in America went for their conductors and from Germany came usually the conductors who were charged with Wagner's music-dramas and other "serious" work in American opera houses. An Italian might do very well with the operas of his own country; a French conductor might at least have his routine uses; but for "real" conducting in the "high" sense of the word there could be only a German. This last remnant of the Teutonic tradition endured long in our opera houses and concert halls. Then it became limp, faded, threadbare. For there came fifteen years or more ago to the Metropolitan Opera House in New York a conductor of the first rank, known to many another city besides, an Italian, Arturo

Toscanini. For five years he did much of the "serious work" of the opera house; for five years he led impressively in one and another of Wagner's music-dramas—a grievous blow to the tradition; and then, at last, for final thrust into its very bowels, he proved little less impressive in symphonic music when he undertook a concert now and then as conductor of the Metropolitan orchestra.

When Mr. Toscanini came first to the Metropolitan, the wiseacres wagged their heads ominously, and those who were prone to mistake Teutonic prejudices for lofty principles made the same boding motions. Who was this Toscanini, with a great reputation behind him in South America and Italy—lands in which such a reputation could not—or at any rate should not—be made? First of all, he conducted absolutely from memory and he had always done so. Report ran that he carried the scores of countless operas, and to the last minutiæ of detail, in an abnormally susceptible and retentive memory. Gossip told how, within a week, he could so absorb the music and the text of a most intricate modern music-drama, poring over it at the piano, reading and rereading it for hours and for whole nights at a time, until it was photographed upon his memory—yet not merely photographed, but visualized there as a living and communicable thing. He had so carried twenty-two operas in his head in one season; he could recall as many more with a little study. Singers and players who had worked with him bore unanimous testimony to the completeness and the accuracy of Mr. Toscanini's memorizing. He knew the smallest details of the music or the composer's glosses upon it. He knew every line of the text and the stage directions. He had corrected out of easy recollection errors in parts that had escaped his most meticulous predecessors.

And lo! it was all true. He did so conduct when he appeared first at the Metropolitan. He has so conducted ever since. He conducted so again when he passed to symphonic music as conductor, on occasion, of the Metropolitan orchestra and when he lately traversed America as conductor of the newly assembled orchestra of the Teatro alla Scala of Milan.

At the Metropolitan when he took in hand a new production, a fresh revival, or even the preparation of a repertory piece for which he was to be responsible for the first time, never in the whole history of the opera house had rehearsals been so thorough. Mr. Toscanini came to them with not only the whole opera—music and drama alike—in his head, but with as clear an image of what in every direction he would achieve with it. He schooled his orchestra not only as a body, but choir by choir, sometimes almost instrument by instrument. He counseled the singers in their parts not only at rehearsals, but for hours in private study in their rooms. ' He received the chorus from the thorough preliminary preparation of one of his lieutenants and then worked with it as with his orchestra. He had a keen eye, a fertile imagination, a quickness and sureness of expedient with settings and lighting, with the whole ordering of the stage. Separately he worked at each element in the production of an opera until every one concerned in it was thoroughly prepared in his individual share and in his coöperation with others. Then, in the final rehearsals, he coördinated all these elements—orchestra, chorus, singing-players, the illusion of the stage, the whole music, the whole drama—into the unit of the image he had reasoned, imagined and kept in his mind from the start.

If Mr. Toscanini was unsparing to all his forces, he spared himself even less. If he would not rest until the last detail of preparation had been assured, the result—in such unified, complete and polished performances as the Metropolitan had not hitherto known—justified him. Since Seidl's time no conductor there had so stamped himself upon the operas that he undertook. None, either, had accomplished so much with them, and they ranged from Gluck's "Orpheus" and "Armide" to Dukas's "Ariane" and Verdi's "Otello"; from Wagner's "Tristan" to Wolf-Ferrari's "Donne Curiose." In spite of the wiseacres, the impression spread that these were the ways of an operatic conductor of the first rank and that these were the results such a conductor accomplished—though he did happen to be an Italian.

For Mr. Toscanini, seemingly, conducting, and particularly orchestral conducting, is primarily self-expression. Obviously none but him knows the purposes and the processes with which he approaches a piece of music and finally brings it to performance; while, unless he is different from most conductors, he himself may hardly be conscious of them. Clearly, however, by the evidence of the concert-hall, he is not of those who would first discover the composer's thought, emotion, procedure, idiosyncrasy, and then bear them to the audience as fully as they may. Of course, this transmission does take more or less color from the transmitter and his means—that is to say, from the mind and spirit of the conductor and the quality of his orchestra; but within these limits, there is such a thing as objective conducting. In contrast Mr. Toscanini seems almost wholly subjective. What he would exhibit to his hearers, impress upon them, infuse into them, is his own reaction to the music in hand. The composer and the composition fall into second place; the orchestra becomes no more than a responsive and imparting instrument; the conductor is "the be-all and the end-all" of the hour; the audience listens to him, answers to him, while upon its perceptions and sensibilities, he veritably plays. The prelude to Wagner's "Tristan," the soliloquy of Isolde, dying and transfigured, flood Mr. Toscanini with emotion. Through the music and the orchestra he outpours that emotion upon a whole concert-room. From Beethoven's symphony in C minor he receives certain sensations. Those sensations, raised to white heat in the fire of performance, he drives home upon his hearers. To the last inflection he makes the orchestra his voice.

First of all, as every great conductor must, Mr. Toscanini conducts with the clearly apprehending, the firmly designing and the finely discriminating mind. He does not merely memorize his music. He grasps its substance until he has made it a part, a living part, of himself. Through and through he knows it largely and knows it minutely. Comprehending it so, he can preserve its unity. Each detail, and each accenting of a detail, falls into its due place, sometimes insignificant, sometimes salient. For Mr. Toscanini discriminates as he conducts. He does not magnify the unimportant or make the important monotonous. There are middle voices and middle shadings in his conducting. It does not alternate heights and depths in fictitious contrasts. In every composition he practices the science of musical architecture and then by imagination and feeling warms it into an art. To "sit under him" is to hear the art of musical design practiced as no other conductor now practices it. Incredible as it may seem, an Italian conductor may have intellect. To intellect Mr. Toscanini adds imagination, the finely subjective imagination that no other conductor in America has possessed in such degree as he. It is the divining and individualizing imagination that is the highest attribute of a great conductor.

II. Many-Sided Muck

One sort of conductor, like Mr. Toscanini, invites his hearers to receive his impressions of the music that he chooses, to listen to Mozart or Beethoven, Tschaikowsky or d'Indy, after it has passed through his temperament. He plays upon his men as some pianists play upon their instruments in order that the orchestra may express himself quite as much as the composer whose name stands upon the program. Those of another sort regard themselves as only means to an end—and that end is the clearest and fullest communication of the contents of the music in hand as the composer wrought and felt it. These conductors approach a given piece, be it a simple symphony by Haydn or an intricate tone-poem by Strauss, with an eye single to its peculiar traits. They apprehend its structure, assimilate its substance, penetrate its moods, assort and adjust its details to the underlying or dominating musical and poetic content, discover its accent and eloquence, and then to their utmost seek to communicate all these things to their hearers. They differentiate each piece that they undertake from all the rest. They give to each its individual voice.

Dr. Muck, when he graced the Boston Orchestra, was such a one. He sought only the substance, the spirit, the peculiar life of the music as it came from the composer's hand. His personal distinction was to be impersonal before his music, but not impersonal in the negative sense. Rather, he had as many personalities as there were composers and pieces on his programs. He made himself and his orchestra the eloquent and the characterizing voice of each. No conductor of our time has seemed to have so few limitations of sympathetic understanding and answering emotion.

The secret of this discrimination, this truly interpretative quality, this self-subordination, lies, perhaps, in the qualities of Dr. Muck as man no less than as musician. His work has proved him a man of strong and fine intellect, of alert, nervous and sensitive mind. He was schooled in the liberal studies; he knows other arts than the one that he practices; he has lived in the world of cultivated men and not merely in the world of makers of music; he looks upon life shrewdly and humorously. He has the penetrating, discriminating and orderly mind that springs from mental discipline and mental training. He understands before he feels, and the breadth and the fineness of his understanding he has proved from Bach through the composers of our own particular place and hour. But mental qualities alone make only a dry conductor. He must have emotional understanding and responsiveness as well. On this score, again as his work has proved him, Dr. Muck is no less finely strung. His is the alert, sensitive, nervous spirit that enters into the moods and the emotions of the symphony, the tone-poem, or the concert piece before him, and that seizes and reflects them vividly and vitally. As he has proved time and again, he is sensitive alike to the varied poetry, the varied drama, the whole range of the expressive quality of music. He has kept it an emotional speech. Such a union of mental and emotional qualities does not in itself round a conductor. He must add to them the intrinsically musical qualities—the feeling for beauty and poignancy of tone, for musical design and form and ornament, for the underlying and distinguishing melody, for the songful utterance, for the charm and the power of ordered sound. Dr. Muck knew no less this purely musical sensitiveness. He is the man of intellect, the man of feeling, who has found the conducting of music the normal and instinctive outlet for these qualities. His mental, emotional and musical traits stood ever in even balance.

By general consent, the Boston Orchestra under Dr. Muck was the incomparable orchestra of the world. His purpose was to make it as perfect an instrument as he could compass. He would not have it merely more eloquent than other orchestras; for that, however high the standard, is relatively a common criterion. He would have it eloquent with the rare and ideal eloquence in which fulfillment matches vision. To that end he shaped his programs and ordered his rehearsals. For that end he lavished all his powers tirelessly and stimulated all the powers of his men. They answered as though they knew and felt the goal. At the close of his long last term in Boston the orchestra stood at the apogee of attainment. It was as perfect an instrument as a human instrument could well be. It was perfect in the range, the balance, the euphony, the elasticity, and the sensibility of the blended tonal mass; perfect in the luminous utterance of music; in the manifold force of voice that it yielded, in diverse richness and coloring, in the variety of its march, in rhythmic suppleness and felicity, in its eloquence of mood and passion, image and suggestion, poetry and drama. The orchestra was a virtuoso orchestra in the highest sense of the word. It was even more than a virtuoso orchestra because it warmed its virtuosity with glowing beauty and winged it with the multifold strength of ordered and sensitive powers. It delighted the ear, it transported the imagination. Its voice was an emotion in itself. They say that the old and dying Vieuxtemps sent for the young Ysaye that he might hear one of his violin concertos played as he had imagined it. So more than one composer, of old or newly dead, might have been fain to summon the Boston Orchestra under Dr. Muck to hear it play his music. The fortunate living came and heard for themselves and departed rejoicing. In their hearts they may have even said: "Did I really write so?"

It is perilous to bear the measuring rule to the orchestral Olympus. But surely it is safe to say that no living conductor has assembled in himself more of the attributes of a great conductor or held them in juster balance than Dr. Muck. *Servans servorum Dei*—the servant of the servants of God—the early Popes used to proudly call themselves. So Dr. Muck might have called himself the servant of the composers whose music he played. He transmitted music to us in the living image of its form and substance, in the voice and in the emotion, as it seemed, in which it was created. Divining, he imparted. Imparting, he enhanced and intensified. For in him is that faculty of divination and that quality of impartment which differentiates the great conductor from the merely able practitioner of his art. The composer writes in emotion, sometimes in an emotion that the music hardly embodies and releases. Divining, penetrating, Dr. Muck enters into this emotion, transmits it, and sometimes releases and heightens it as though he were freeing that, which from sheer intensity of feeling, holds the composer almost tongue-tied. As widely as these composers range, so ranges Dr. Muck's divination. And to do and to be these things is to be a very great conductor.

III. Mengelberg and Melodrama

Mr. Mengelberg has become the most sought of "prima donna" conductors. He does not venture outside of symphonic and choral music and the more, then, has Europe sought him for such concerts from London to Petrograd. Now he is come to America, first as visiting conductor of the lately defunct National Symphony Orchestra and again to share with Mr. Stransky the conductorship of the Philharmonic Society. By common consent Mr. Mengelberg ranks high in his profession, applauded in his native Holland, in adjacent Germany, and, most of all, in Paris. His energy is inexhaustible; journeying has become second nature to him; he is a quick but exacting drill-master; he has the classic and the modern repertory at his fingers' ends; he is a conductor of both individuality and power.

Mr. Mengelberg conducts lustily, with all his heart and all his soul—and also all.his body. His right hand beats the measure with exceeding clearness, firmness and precision. His left, no less, is seldom in repose and even then, it must be caressing his cheek, so used is he to making some use of it. With his left hand he does not signal instrument or group of instruments, as most conductors do. He does that apparently by the concentration of his glance upon them or by inward reliance upon the players' close following of the score. Usually with his left hand he is writing the contours of the melody upon the air, flinging out emphases, catching and concentrating climaxes, like the old pictures of Jove in the classical dictionaries with a fist full of thunderbolts, or else holding the orchestra in the hollow of his palm, as it were, in a moment of transition.

By these tokens, Mr. Mengelberg is a conductor who seeks large and emphatic effect out of whatever music he undertakes, who relies upon sharp contrasts, who spends little pains upon exposition and the refinements of expression, and who is insensitive to the middle gradients of power. Being so minded, he hoists the finale of Beethoven's Fifth Symphony for example, from plane to plane of excited jubilation, holding the music and the orchestra momentarily suspended in his Jove-like fist for some gentler and contrasting measures. Being so minded, he also takes the slow movement of that same symphony with a robustness that does violence to its imaginative and capricious quality and that insistently coarsens it. In similar fashion, the gentler, the feminine melody as it were, of the first allegro hardly finds its voice. No sooner does it appear than Mr. Mengelberg sends the first masculine melody crashing down upon its head, even though the music so loses all quality of contrast.

Yet when the contrast can be emphatic, Mr. Mengelberg delights to magnify it. By this time, nearly every one knows the sublimity of the first measures of Strauss's "Zarathustra"—the long-held, dark and surging organ point, the flaming trumpets, the resilient and resplendent strings, the mighty flood of tone that flings Zarathustra in the sunrise forth upon the world and the problem of living. Mr. Mengelberg is powerful with it; he would pile every orchestral richness upon it; he would make the tone of his band like a great, free, releasing voice. Then ensues, in the tone-poem, the passage of "The Back-World's Men"—chromatic, crabbed and dun. Mr. Mengelberg seizes such a contrast and drives it into the imaginations of his hearers. Similarly, just before the beginning of the exuberant close of the overture to "Der Freischütz" he must almost choke the orchestra into concentrated suspense that it may blaze forth into the brilliancy of the coda.

It is so, too, with Mr. Mengelberg's measuring of the quality of tone that he draws from his men. He would have it very soft and very shadowed—and no conductor can achieve a more exquisite pianissimo—as in the beginning of this same overture. Or he would have it at the other extreme of power, brilliancy and elasticity as in the "Dance Song" of "Zarathustra." Between he seldom finds middle voices, shaded colors, subtle accents. Whatever he does, he must do at the highest of intensities, each in its kind. Of course these diverse intensities are highly exciting and highly obvious. They have as manifestly their limitations. They make Mr. Mengelberg a conductor in terms of melodrama.

IV. Monteux the Visualist

In Boston, succeeding Dr. Muck, after the half-forgotten interregnum of Rabaud, now dwells the ablest of the Parisian conductors—Pierre Monteux. Of them, young or old, he only has escaped the rut in which orchestral concerts in Paris live, move and fulfill their dull being. From this openness of mind, from this eager, assimilating curiosity spring programs that in catholicity of choice, range forward and range backward, freedom from every sort of prejudice are unequaled in Europe or America. Mr. Monteux is a widely read musician who adds incessantly to his reading; wherever new men rise writing in new manner, thither he turns an inquiring and usually a welcoming ear. He has the wisdom to perceive that the most enduring classics are staled by too frequent repetition; that the routine of familiarity may dull even a masterpiece. Hence a wholesome discretion with the "standard repertory"; and persistent and often fruitful search for overlooked music of established composers. Scarcely a conductor in the exacting task of program-making better assorts the old with the new; the immediately interesting with the permanently valuable; the demands of the day with the scope of the years. To an open, assimilating mind, he owes again his quick perception of American standards in symphonic concerts, his sense of the public they assemble, his ready conformity to the ways of a new world. Possibly, too, such a plastic temperament gives him his firm yet elastic grasp upon practical orchestral affairs. Each of the preceding conductors of the Boston Orchestra, except such a mere stop-gap as Rabaud, served it well. None has served it better than Mr. Monteux, saving it from dissolution, re-forming, re-practicing, restoring it, when secession threatened it—and all this as the one, the inevitable thing to do.

As conductor, Mr. Monteux excels with music dependent for impression upon play of rhythm and vibrancy of color, music also of romantic content or dramatic movement. He has gathered long experience as conductor of the Russian Ballet with mimes and dancers, long experience in opera houses with singers and stage. Out of this experience, he brings into the concert-hall the objective, the visualizing sense. He cherishes the large, keen, direct impression upon his hearers. Modern and ultra-modern music of the dance, as Ravel or Stravinsky has written it, quickens him. Romantic music of the nineteenth century—of Weber, Berlioz, Liszt—similarly spurs him. With both, he seems to visualize progress and illusion as he might, and did, with the opera and ballet in his years in the theater. He is equally eloquent with classics inviting such treatment—the overtures, the Fifth and the Seventh Symphonies of Beethoven; while to the other German masters—say Brahms, Schumann, Schubert, Mendelssohn—he brings warm feeling and sensitive ear to instrumental melody. He bears home to his hearers Schumann's romantic exuberance and moodiness. He revitalizes Mendelssohn; his is a luminous rather than a rugged and abstruse Brahms. Only eighteenth-century music occasionally evades him; since with it his hand is not always quick and supple to shade, since too often he chooses the square-cut period. There, however, he seldom fails to interest; while like all conductors of the Boston symphony concerts he has steadily ripened under both the freedom and the exactions that are their standards. It is not Mr. Monteux's way to blaze for a day; he prefers the steady, the cumulative glow.

V. The Songful Stock

They say in Chicago that now and then Mr. Stock fancies his audience saying to itself at sight of his presence, familiar these many years, and at sound of his orchestra's voice: "There he is again." The dread need not haunt him. For although the Chicago Orchestra comes too seldom to Eastern concert-halls, when it does come its worth speaks for itself; while as clear is the quality of its conductor, Frederick Stock.

His band is as clear-minded and quick to his will as was Dr. Muck's of old in Boston or Mr. Toscanini's Milanese of nearer memory. As for many a year and to the finer and more enduring credit, Mr. Stock, conducting, is all for the music and not at all for himself. Hence no conscious or unconscious assertion of "personality" upon hearers; no displayful exercises in the concert-room. In his study, he peruses and penetrates a piece in hand; in rehearsal he prepares it and the orchestra for performance. In public, he has only to reassert his will upon the orchestra, to resummon the composer to voice. His large and flowing beat seems of the simplest; his left hand restrains oftener than urges, sets no spirals upon a throbbing air. Within, but firm upon both band and audience, is the force that plumbs the depths of orchestral song, gains the heights of orchestral sonority. As he proves in the first movement of Rakhmaninov's Symphony and again in the Finale, or in the final surge of Isolde's death-song, Mr. Stock excels in the advance and recession, the suspensive stay, the sustained flood, the deep-laid foundation while the surface boils, which is the conductor's art of climax. As he proves in the Russian's Adagio and upon many another neighboring page, he commands equally unfolding, intensifying, ascending instrumental melody. He chooses the pace that reveals it; knows the long gradient that is mounting path; feels the modulation accenting and diversifying progress; holds phrase to phrase in unbroken undulation; keeps background as warm as line is clear.

Finely, too, he differentiates and characterizes melody. So to discover the song of symphonic music and enfold his hearers therein, so to ply symphonic climax and sweep listeners upon it is to be eloquent, masterful conductor. For the most distinctive quality in Mr. Stock is his ability to bear orchestra and audience deep into the music, to hold them fast within its voice, progress, spirit.

Accessory virtues are many. As a whole, Mr. Stock hears and feels the music in hand, regardful of unity, nowhere sparing pains. Many a conductor, having wrenched the prelude of "Tristan" from the voice of fate into the voice of desire, having gained the climax of that ceaseless longing, lets the rest slide "any old way" into the measures of Isolde's soliloquy. Mr. Stock perceives and conveys the descent of that music, sated, numb, wearing itself into silence and nothingness. However ear and imagination may hear the content of Rakhmaninov's Symphony it is no mean design in tones. Clear-minded, plastic of hand with such architecture, Mr. Stock maintains the large ascent, the structural unity. He is as sedulous with the proportions of orchestral tone; he seeks and gains its sustained richness; its momentary incisiveness within his own ears, upon the ears of his audience. Few conductors achieve better than he—and his orchestra with him—the depth and glow of Rakhmaninov's or Wagner's harmonies. They are according to his own mind, heart and time. As he adjusts details like threads into a fabric, so does he discover and intensify the outstanding strand.

Mr. Stock can make an orchestra, a music flash. Only one shortcoming persists in him. Discerning and practiced conductor, he heeds rhythm. Once and again, as in the Scherzo or the Finale of Rakhmaninov's symphony, he makes it beat high. Whenever the composer wills, he sustains it. But to his younger hearers, perhaps overswayed by a custom and a pleasure of the day, often comes the wish that he would sharpen, intensify, whirl with it.

VI. Stokowski's Progress

Of the younger conductors now working in America, Mr. Stokowski is unquestionably the best equipped, the fullest tested. Surface shortcomings he once had in a certain displayful attitude toward his audiences, which he has nearly outgrown; in a certain inclination toward social prestige which, again, he may discover in the long run, is a vain thing. As conductor there is no mistaking his ability with romantic music of any period or any school, with the pieces of the moderns and the ultra-moderns, with whatever is sharply rhythmed, warmly colored, variously impassioned, largely voiced. In all such music he conducts with imagination and eloquence, vividly designing, ardently projecting, with flashes of rare insight, with strokes of clear power. Finesse and elegance may still somewhat elude him with the eighteenth-century masters; his severer classics may lack a measure of poise, may miss grave and deep intensities; but Mr. Stokowski still stands in the waxing years. Moreover, as he has amply proved in Philadelphia, his standards of orchestral technique are high; while he can gradually impose them upon his forces. When he first took over the Philadelphia Orchestra and for an appreciable period thereafter, it was a mediocre band. Now it plays with a precision, pliancy, fluency and balance of tone, with a vitality of rhythm, a roundness of period, a pervading warmth and resilience that are surely Mr. Stokowski's handiwork upon it.

Latterly no orchestra in the United States has gained so much in prestige as that which Mr. Stokowski leads. For years he has been gradually bettering the personnel and the playing of the band; for years he has been ripening himself as conductor. Now, as the way is with such progress, the outcome seems suddenly to stand clear. At home in Philadelphia, in New York and in the other cities that the orchestra regularly or occasionally visits, it has been more applauded and better supported than ever before. The expert have found new and lively interests in its concerts, while less exacting hearers have drawn fresh pleasure and stimulation from them. From many a side it is possible to hear warm praise, to discover a new respect for the Philadelphia Orchestra. Especially among musicians, "it is in the air" as the phrase goes, that the

Philadelphian band is the risen orchestra in America. For that very reason, it is beginning to attract individual players of a quality that it has much needed. Before long, if it can finally escape one and another hampering condition of the past, it bids fair to be the orchestra that Mr. Stokowski deserves. At last Philadelphia, like Boston and Chicago, is tasting the sweets of pride in an orchestra that has given the city prestige in the arts.

By the tokens of recent seasons Mr. Stokowski and Mr. Monteux are now the most interesting conductors of symphonic music in America. Mr. Stock, Mr. Damrosch, Mr. Stransky, are now fixed quantities, little likely to change; Mr. Mengelberg, too, is what he is; Mr. Gabrilowitsch and Mr. Ysaye are relatively at the beginning of their careers as conductors by profession. Not one of these, unless it is Mr. Gabrilowitsch, has the personal distinction, the individualizing force and quality of Mr. Stokowski. To none of them do audience and orchestra more clearly react. Whether the listener agrees or disagrees with his version of a particular piece, it is not possible to hear it and him with indifferent ears. Whatever the number in hand, he strikes the fire that gives vitality to the music and individuality to the performance. He commands at need the delicate or the puissant hand. He conducts plastically and with imagination. His ear measures the tone of his orchestra while his spirit kindles it. He designs as well as colors. He is open-minded to any and all deserving music; he has the characterizing faculty when he plays it. New years and widening opportunity have still to deepen and to refine these qualities, but, as they stand now, they set Mr. Stokowski high among the leaders of American orchestras. He has overcome or put by not a few of his earlier infirmities and in that self-mastery is best proof of his new quality and place.

VII. Stransky and Strife

Temperance is not the distinguishing grace of either the eulogists or the detractors of Mr. Stransky. Those who admire him ardently aver that he is one of the foremost of living conductors. His detractors rush as far in the other direction. In their ears, Mr. Stransky has not a merit in the concert-room; he is the merest charlatan among conductors, which is much too arrogant and sweeping an assertion to persuade those of us who try to keep fair and open minds about music and musicians as about all things else. Moreover, harping upon a man's "sincerity," like most speculation about motives that we do not know at first hand, is a ticklish business and may be left as one of the "extra-hazardous" pastimes of the young.

As usual, the workaday truth probably lies somewhere between the two extremes. Mr. Stransky is not a Nikisch or a Muck or a Toscanini. No more is he a conductor to be dismissed with a petulant sneer. How capable and thorough a drill master he is, the Philharmonic Society, under him, has clearly shown. For its old massive exactness Mr. Stransky substituted the elastic precision with which it now plays either under his own or a visiting conductor's baton. It plays with euphony in the several choirs and in the whole orchestra, with rhythmic suppleness and vitality or with diversity of appropriate tone. Throughout, the wood-wind choir and the horns are good to hear and virtuosi clearly sit among them. The strings have gained in suavity and luminosity of tone and in capacity for instrumental song, though they have never become edgeless and shimmering. The old Philharmonic was a band of power and little else; now the tradition has yielded in every choir except the brass, which still overdrives itself or is overdriven.

By so much Mr. Stransky has served the Philharmonic Society and its public well, and by so much he proves that he has a hand and ear for the finer distinctions of orchestral playing. He has his feeling for the subtler qualities of music, too, as he often shows, and for such strokes of tonal eloquence as the celebrated entrance of the horns toward the end of Strauss's "Don Juan." Indeed, the playing of the tone-poem, more than of any other piece, exemplifies Mr. Stransky's dominant qualities as a conductor. He is all for the "effect" that shall play on the instant and unmistakably upon the susceptibilities of his hearers. He would keep them, as it seems, at a high pitch of nervous excitement. He would bathe them in his tonal sonorities, sting them with his rhythms, sweep them along in the irresistible current of the music or else cradle them sensuously in its sentiment. So he and his orchestra fling off "Don Juan" and twenty telling details and as many more glories of the suffusing orchestral color go by the board; so he can make the march of the magic brooms in Dukas's scherzo a thing of fearsome sonorities and cumulating beat. Where he falls short is in the sensitive modulation of his music by the fine instinct and imagination that dwell in conductors of the first rank and in the subtlety—and also the truth—that makes an "effect" seem not an effect, but the inevitable and irresistible voice of the music of the moment.

II

SINGING-ACTORS

1. Garden—Mirror of the Moderns

PICK, if you will, twenty technical flaws in Mary Garden's singing. Discover, as it is easy to discover, that hers was originally a voice that might have served admirably the purposes of song. She has preferred to make it an exalting, emotional, characterizing and delineative speech. To that end she uses all her vocal resources; for it she will risk any vocal sacrifice, attempt any vocal distortion. The technician will rage at her; singing-teachers count her the abomination of desolation—in their trade; while sensitive ears, trained to the older arts of pure song, in and out of the opera houses, do writhe now and then under the quality of some of her tones and the methods by which she gains them. But she attains no less her real end. Her singing is the speech of the part she is playing. In her tones float the traits and the emotions of the character portrayed. She colors them with every change and process of mood, with every subtlety of suggestion. Hers is a truly magnetic art, the art of the singing-actress, however uneven she may be in the exemplification of it, near its fullness. Hers are modern means to modern ends. With her came a new day in operatic acting and singing.

Miss Garden's singing—or oftener declamation—calls to a more vivid life than any other singing-actress now may, the Thaïs of Alexandrian feasts and the desert convent; the Louise of Montmartre the day before yesterday; the little juggler whom the Virgin loved; the piteous Mélisande, or the tempestuous and brooding Carmen. Her range is wide and she differentiates each of the characters she chooses from it. The heavy-lidded, panther-like Oriental girl, who has thought the thoughts of passion and first feels it when the white-shouldered Jokanaan comes from Herod's pit, is far indeed from the Mélisande, wisp in the wind of fate, trembling to the impulses she hardly knows, moving, living as the vision of a dream. Louise of the dressmaker's shop, palpitating to the surge and the heat of Paris, is no less remote from the little white monk, who sits apart and downcast in the common room and wonders how he, too,—poor juggler lad—shall make his works serve Our Lady. To differentiate and to individualize her characters, to call them, each in its kind, to as intense life as is her own is Miss Garden's chief purpose. And the chief means is the exalted speech that music gives her when such imagination, such communicating emotional force and such self-surrender as are hers, may color her tones.

No one quite knows the voice of Mary Garden; but her hearers know the voices of Louise, of Thaïs, of Mélisande and of Salome. She is less the actress who happens also to sing (as Whistler said Leighton "also" painted) than the actress who has discovered that music affords a more imparting and thrilling speech. She is as vivid in her appeal to the eye. Consider Thaïs with her train of dancing and singing girls sweeping into Nicias's house in the exuberant joy of careless and sensuous life; Mélisande still and dreaming in the pale sunshine of the terrace by the empty sea, and with eyes that search its emptiness; Louise rapt in the intoxication of the Paris that spreads the elation of living at her feet; Salome crouching over the silent cistern, whither the executioner has descended; when even Strauss's orchestra makes stillness searching and expectant. Of such are the unforgettable images that Miss Garden summons to the eye and the imagination of her audiences that her characters may live before them. They live, most of all, because of the superb and tireless vitality of the singing-actress behind them. Life—the joy of it, the exertion of it, the reward of it, the pleasure daily renewed of all these things—burns too brightly and too eagerly in Mary Garden for her impersonations to be one whit less alive than is she. Even when she exceeds and overemphasizes as with Fiora in "The Love of Three Kings," or distorts as with Monna Vanna in Février's music-drama after Maeterlinck, she errs with a certain magnificence.

Miss Garden is the guardian, in America, of the living and vivid "tradition" of the ultra modern opera. It is her knowledge that directs, her spirit that informs whatever is accomplished in this country in the renewal, from time to time, of the beauty and the power of the music into which Debussy has wrought Maeterlinck's "Pélléas and Mélisande." Each hearer of the opera listens for himself. Some there are whom the comparative newness of the idiom of the music baffles until they lose themselves in the pursuit of Debussy's harmonies, progressions, modulations, scales and rhythms. They debate of the details of his musical speech as though they were absolute and exact things and not means to a particular end of expression. They inquire whether such speech may serve other composers and other music-dramas —a matter of pure and futile conjecture. They do serve Maeterlinck's play, and beyond that purpose Debussy had no occasion to go. So Miss Garden's means as singing-actress serve the ends of the opera. Within music that so speaks the spirits of the personages of the play; that stirs with the fate that creeps about them, the singing players must seem the figures of Maeterlinck's dream and Debussy's music. So, indeed, does Miss Garden wholly vanish into the being that she would simulate. So she speaks with the very tones of Debussy's music. So she quivers and swims, pales and brightens in its very atmosphere.

II. The Fervors of Farrar

Geraldine Farrar is not now the exquisitely voiced singing-actress that she once was. A streak of vulgarity, of showiness for its own sake, has gradually crept into her singing and her acting. But, like Miss Garden, she knows the *joie de vivre;* she possesses a rich and glowing vitality and she imparts it to whatever she undertakes in the opera house and even in the moving-picture "studio." On the speaking stage, it is easy to believe, she could also act. Miss Farrar has histrionic imagination, diversity, range and resource. She is capable of vivid operatic passion and "states of soul." Her tones—except in the upper range where they now and then turn a little thin, shrill, pale—have fullness, surety, warmth. Operatic comedy and operatic tragedy—if it be not too heroic or too sublimated—are at her command. She has a quick and clear, if often deliberately bizarre, sense of pictorial effect in the theater. Her preparation of her parts is thorough and her ambition was once ceaseless.

Miss Farrar's Carmen takes high place among the Carmens of our stage. Her Tosca has many of the virtues of Mme. Bernhardt's in the theater—a Tosca that is hot with Latin intensities and changeful with quick-coming Latin passions. She excels in Puccini's "Madama Butterfly." The spirit and not the surface of Butterfly animates her acting of the part, and transforms a pathetically sentimental drama into a piercing poetic tragedy. At first she erred with her Butterfly in the pursuit of a sham and superfluous Japanese realism. Now, and in the scenes with Pinkerton in the first act in particular, she has lifted and refined her impersonation to an idealized and a very poignant beauty. The exotic setting fades and Cho-Cho-San ceases to be the Geisha of Nagasaki and becomes the image of all women who have given their souls, when men wanted only their bodies, and wanted these only until it was time to ride away. Through the second and the third acts, Miss Farrar's original impersonation was vivid with significant histrionic strokes and piteous with the emotions of which her tones were the living voice. She deployed all the musical and histrionic elements that she has now fused into a whole that almost to the end of the opera sustains itself at a height of tragic beauty and tragic intensity. She continues to idealize the girl into the poetic and romantic beauty that she has sought in the first act. At the same time she keeps the searchingly human truth, the wringing human intensity of Butterfly's fate and emotions. She accomplishes all these things by the fused arts of the singing-actress—the heightened expressiveness of her musical speech now to beauty and now to poignancy and now to both, and the histrionic action that is as the visualization of the character, the moment, the emotion and the music itself.

Within these limits of Butterfly, Miss Farrar fulfills, and idealizes, all that a singing-actress may do, and with the beauty, the felicity and the intensity of her artistry, at once ordered and spontaneous, she warms the minds, kindles and sways the imaginations, and wrings the hearts of those that see and hear. Out of Miss Farrar's incarnation of Madama Butterfly the new art of the music-drama of our time, the new art of operatic impersonation, clothes Puccini's music and Long's story, becomes Belasco's play. The music is mannered, sentimentalized, drenched in the composer's instinct for the effective theater. Under the thin exotic veneer, the fable is akin to the music. Upon both, from Miss Farrar as singing actress, falls the finer vesture of universal human tragedy.

The bizarre, the showy, the vulgar, but, at the same time, the deep-seated human side of Miss Farrar best exemplifies itself in her acting of one of her recent parts, the Zaza of Berton and Belasco's play and of Leoncavallo's hitherto moribund opera. The music, falling within easy compass of her tones, unexacting upon her vocal skill, leaves her unhampered in characterization of the personage, in projection of mood and intensifying of emotion. She can be as showy as one of her instincts prompts her to be in the dressing-room of the café-concert; every pose, gesture, intonation may reek of Zaza's world. The more bizarre the means and outcome, the fuller the flavor and in such a part Miss Farrar would have her operatic characterization "high." The opera proceeds along familiar course of such "contraptions" of the stage and, almost within the hour, the singing-actress is the repentant, the illumined, the transformed Zaza touched to the heart by the music of a child, putting away old sins for new graces. Frank mechanics, hackneyed sentimentalism, pseudo-emotion of the theater that Réjane herself could not quite clothe with human quality. And lo! out of Miss Farrar's song and action rises image of human woman prey to human emotions, conquering herself in human resolution. The Roman forgave much to one who had loved much. No less may be forgiven Miss Farrar because no less she humanizes—not Zaza merely, but almost every one of her personages.

III. Jeritza: Fused and Rounded

When an astronomer discovers a new-found comet, he probably sees it more vividly than in the nights when he is calculating its orbit, weighing its gases, preparing it generally for scientific catalogue. Similarly, though Marie Jeritza has as yet traversed the stage of the Metropolitan Opera House through only a few months and there taken no more than five parts, the years to come will confirm and assort rather than widen and deepen the impressions of audiences. They have seen, and will continue to see, her as a woman tall, blond, lithe and lovely as any Nordic ideal. They have heard her as a singer in whose voice dwell sensuous beauty, vibrant power and transforming color multifold. They have discovered her as an actress whose declamation and song are a speech of trait, thought, and mood as the drama projects them. They have found her an actress whose pose may crystallize for the instant a personage or a passion. They have contrasted the static, solitary, remote illusion of her Sieglinde—daughter of a god yet still half woman—with the changeful fires, the quivering stresses of her Tosca—above all else daughter of the theater. Side by side, they have set the tremulous sensibility of her Elsa, wistful, iridescent, dreamlike; the sharp contours, the hard surfaces, the shrill-strung emotions of her actress in "The Dead City;" her primitive, earthy Santuzza in "Cavalleria Rusticana." Out of all these impressions and in their own workaday vernacular, Mme. Jeritza's audiences count her a "personality"—the first, perhaps, in the general view, to pass the threshold of the Metropolitan since Miss Farrar crossed the great room of Capulet's house in a "Romeo and Juliet" of 1906.

Agree with the purists that cheapening usage has made of "personality" a label common, trite, variously meaningless; yet no other better contains the sum of Mme. Jeritza as singing-actress. No doubt it is the obligation of reviewing to analyze and assort, but to enumerate her abilities is by no means to convey their commingled quality. 1, 2, 3, 4, 5, 6, is each an individual and significant number; but they must be marshaled and pronounced together to make one hundred and twenty-three thousand four hundred and fifty-six. Presumably there are connoisseurs in the beauty of women quite content to look upon Mme. Jeritza, lustrous as gold in face and locks, plastic as mercury in flow of limb and torso. Others are as pleased to hear her lambent tones, to note the color playing aptly and endlessly over them, to feel the imaginative and propulsive instinct inflecting and winging them. Yet others are deeply and variously moved because of a sudden—and thereafter until the opera is done—they see, know and feel in her Wagner's Sieglinde and Elsa, the Tosca of Sardou and Puccini, the Marie of Erich Korngold and—dimly distant—of "Bruges La Morte."

In a word, by the sum of her powers and possessions and projection, Mme. Jeritza upon the stage works deep and manifold illusion. But into the personage of Tosca or Marie, into the character that is Elsa or Sieglinde or Santuzza, enters the personality of Marie Jeritza. And from that merging are born the speech of song, the mirror of face and body, the histrionic definition, the whole means of impression and illusion that convey to us both operatic figure and singing-actress—always through the vesture of her own bright or wistful beauty. Mme. Jeritza, upon the operatic stage, is not one quality, or two or three, however salient. In herself she is the singing-actress fused, welded, rounded. Molten is the illusion.

IV. Renaud—Actor with Tones

As remarkable an impersonation as the comparatively new and glorious art of singing-acting—of acting enhanced by the more exalted and more penetrating speech of music—has achieved in our day was Maurice Renaud's Rigoletto, a performance which stands in memory with Ternina's Isolde, with Calvé's Carmen.

Renaud was not an operatic personality as Jean de Reszké, for example, nakedly was, or as Miss Garden, in spite of her range from Salome and Sapho at one extreme to Mélisande and Grisélidis at the other, insistently is. None of us, who knew Renaud only across the footlights, even though it was an acquaintance of many years, could isolate his personality at all. We knew him vividly, intimately, as the Rigoletto of Verdi's opera, as the Don Juan of Mozart's, as the Mephistopheles of Berlioz—more truly of Goethe—as the Athanäel of "Thaïs," as the Wolfram of "Tannhäuser," as the threefold "malignant force" of "The Tales of Hoffmann." But in each instance he so identified himself with the operatic personage that no chemico-critical process could first dissolve and then crystallize him out of it. The saying used to run in London that there were as many Lord Rosebervs as that nobleman had activities. There were as many Renauds as the singing-actor had characters. The man who split himself into them like the germ of biological process, who gave them what Mr. Shaw would call the Life Force, kept to himself.

So too with Renaud's voice. *Ex pede Herculem. Ex voce* McCormack or Galli-Curci. By their voices they are known. The distinction of Caruso, for another example, was the volume, the splendor, the propulsive force, and the golden mellowness of his tones. Akin, for the other sex, were Mme. Melba's. The distinction of Mme. Tetrazzini was the exquisite brightness, softness and limpid glamour of the finer range of her voice. With twenty other singers it is the sensuous quality of their tones and the easy, pervasive, answering sensation to it that most commends them. Now Renaud's voice was not a big voice and even in its prime it had no golden notes, no sensuous splendors. No one ever praised it, even in those best years, for the mere brightness and softness of its texture. It was never a vibrant voice, in the common sense of generally communicating quality. It could never be overwhelming by its own propulsive force. It began, as it remained, an expressive voice. Fate gives voices; men, by their intelligence, imagination, ambition, industry and artistic conscience, train them in the shaping and the transmission of the tone, in the molding and the adjustment of the musical phrase, in all the niceties and all the suggestions of diction. There are voices that thrill or charm of themselves, and there are voices that stir and allure by what they impart and the manner of the impartment. In this second category lies the truer and finer artistry of song; and through all his career Renaud practiced it with increasing acuteness and resource to steadily finer and more various result. He was the singer by dint of intelligence, imagination and knowledge, as well as by grace of voice and labor; and the longer, therefore, did he remain the singer. Such artistry preserved Mme. Sembrich to unusual length of vocal days. It preserved Renaud even longer.

Because Renaud was so complete, adroit and resourceful in the artistry of song in the narrower, more technical sense, his tones were the surer, finer and more varied in expressive quality. His voice became as the voice of the monk in "Thaïs," of the demon of "The Damnation of Faust," of Don Juan, of Rigoletto, of the mooning minstrel in "Tannhäuser,"—the more illusively because he had the means as well as the will to transform and to color it. His tones bore suggestion of the haunted and the tortured devotee; of the melancholy and fathomless devil; of the finely amorous and finely irresistible cavalier ever eager to savor new loves, and for mental as well as sensuous satisfactions; of the senile malignancy, the passionate affection or the passionate vindictiveness of the jester; of the dreaming and tender knight of the Wartburg—bore all these things so diversely and illusively, because by adroit finesse and not by wrenching violence, he infused them with emotional or characterizing significance. So long as opera is opera, acting within it will have its inescapable drawbacks and limitations. Under the footlights sits the relentless orchestra and at every turn the singer must meet it. Sing he must or sing he ought at whatever cost of facial play. His pace must be as slow as the unfolding of the music, though the zest for histrionic speed quiver within him. Emotional or characteristic as he would make his musical

V. Chaliapin the Mighty

For Chaliapin, as our American world has lately rediscovered him, there are two distinct publics. One, in New York as seat of opera, knows him near and vividly as Boris Godunov in Musorgsky's like-named music-drama; recalls him distantly and dimly, after sixteen years, as the Mephistopheles of Boïto or Gounod, the monstrous or the meeching Don Basilio of Rossini's "Barber." The other, scattered over a thin hinterland nearly operaless, has heard him, unless it have a Russian past, only as a singer of the concert hall. There, as some say, his fellow Russians, though they flock also to the opera house, like better to hear him. No sooner has he come to the platform than, after the Russian manner between audience and artist, they establish an intimate commerce. His broad blond countenance beams with happy promise, his whole massive figure radiates an anticipating readiness and good will. The assembled company responds with salute and welcome, settles into like expectant glow. He names the song that he chooses, since he follows no appointed program; he sings it, passes to another and another still. By this time out of stored memories his hearers have also made their choices. Exuberantly, vociferously, they demand this piece or that. In as large good humor Chaliapin makes reply, conceding, refusing, deferring, until "all in good time" (as he likes to retort) are content. In such process and progress, audience and singer become for the while a buoyantly reciprocal unit. The like of Chaliapin's concerts hardly another singer or audience, west of Russia, may experience.

In a sense in the concert-hall Chaliapin makes momentary miniatures, but in the succession and sum of them he does disclose more variously than in the opera house the range of his characterizing powers and transmitting faculties. For the while —in evening clothes, upon a bare platform, beside a piano, before an audience laid lengthwise through a tunnel rather than circled in concentration about a stage—he becomes the shrewdly, the comically, drunken miller of a song of Dargomijsky; the frenzied fanatic of Rimsky-Korsakov vowing, almost immolating, himself to God in desert waste; the brigand-chief of Rubinstein, scornful even of dooming foes victorious; the sardonic teller of the tale of the flea—to Musorgsky's music—in Brander's Goethian cellar; the duelist with both death and life through Sasnovsky's mordant, carking song. Or forthwith, at the turning of a leaf, he is the sensuous and artful singer, accomplished in all the inflections and shadings of song, making serene and spacious way through the "grand style" of Beethoven's "In Questa Tomba."

For Chaliapin still keeps a bass voice of magnificent sonorities and suavities, may still at will ply the arts and artifices of orthodox song Italianate. By predilection of mind and spirit, by ambition become habit, in quest of manifold human range and deeper humanity of expression, he prefers to use this voice, this skill, as means to concentrated, conveyed, almost visualized characterization. With verse and music in degree aiding, his tones set the scene, impose the atmosphere, summon the personage. They drive all home upon his hearers, for the instant vital, vivid, complete and possessing. The range of these works of Chaliapin in the concert-hall is the range of humanity.

In the opera house, the range and intensity of Chaliapin's characterizing faculties are as broad and deep. And as befits such environment and aids, ampler and more graphic. In twenty parts of Russian opera and music-drama, Western Europeans, whom he has visited but rarely, do not know him. Yet they have the advantage of us beyond the Atlantic, since they have seen and heard him through the smoldering, senile, savagery, the torturing doubts and dreads of Tsar Ivan in Rimsky-Korsakov's "Maid of Pskov"; through the blindly exalted faiths and sacrifices of the apostle of the "Old Believers" in Musorgsky's "Khovanstchina"; through the sombre, corroding, cruelties, the brooding hate with which he clothes and characters—more out of himself than out of the opera—Philip II of Spain in Verdi's "Don Carlos"; through the Don Quixote of universal fantasy and comicality, and of as universal pang and pity that he similarly leads over Massenet's pale pages. Memory of players in theater or opera house is pitifully short. For the while, of the parts in which we Americans at home have known Chaliapin, we remember only that his Mephistopheles, according to Boïto, was nearly naked in the Brocken Scene and that his Basilio, according to Rossini, was spotted and snuffly.

Of his Boris we know more, since Musorgsky's music-drama, established in the repertory of the Metropolitan Opera House, awaited Chaliapin on his recent return to America as it will at all future comings. To have seen him in the scanty scenes in which the usurping Tsar, remorse-ridden, holds the stage—for they are relatively few in this "opera of the Russian people"—is to retain the image of Boris, sumptuous and splendid, prideful, exalted, majestic, crossing the glittering court of the Kremlin on the way to coronation, at once lording and blessing the subject-folk. As clear and full rests the image of the gently paternal Boris in wistful, half-brooding play with his children in the still, close palace-room. Of a sudden rises, beside and against it, the image of the scheming usurper, the conniving murderer, whipped by remorse as by flail in the hand of specter; fleeing, cringing before it; clutching at the old Chouisky as at some warm, familiar, human thing. Or the Boris whose brow already drips with the clammy sweat of death, questioning vain tongues, searching empty air for the solace and salvation that are not. So he dies drained by evil, doomed by fate.

As, through the intensifying lens of Chaliapin, the eye has seen these images, so has the ear heard, in as intensifying a speech of song, the very tongue of Boris and of Musorgsky for him. The few but spacious phrases of the scene of corona-

VI. Caruso—To His Utmost

In this queer operatic world of ours there have been no audiences like those which Caruso assembled because, in truth, there have been no singers like Caruso. A large part of his hearers, whatever he sang, seemed to come from those who regarded him as one of the unique personages of the time, as Paderewski was to be seen and heard among pianists or Mme. Bernhardt among players. This company go to see her though they know not a word of French and barely heed the play when she is off the stage. So they hear Paderewski, though the piano and its "literature" are sealed books to them, and so they heard and saw Caruso, careless of the opera in which he was appearing or of the part that it yielded him. Enough for them that they looked upon him and listened to him.

And what manner of Caruso went they forth to see and to hear? Surely not the Caruso who used to stand four-square to the audience and pour forth his flood of song. But rather the singing-actor who learned, with commendable perseverance, to penetrate the skin of a character, to be personage in the musical drama, and not merely an acclaimed tenor singing this part or that. In the last decade of his service at the Metropolitan Opera House he was no longer the tenor of the "golden voice," enrapturing audiences by the opulence of his mellow and glowing song; for the quality of Caruso's tones and his ways with them much changed with the passing years. As time matured his voice so did it ripen his imagination and develop his means until his tones became the voice of his personage, until he himself entered, perforce, into part and drama. Not for nothing may a singer, though he be as eminent as Caruso, work year after year with Toscanini.

If the old, golden magnificence had somewhat gone out of the singer's voice, tones remained that carried and imparted emotions variously and poignantly, that revealed the personage who was singing, that took color and accent from the moment of the drama, that characterized, delineated, projected. If once the only emotion that the voice provoked was of the sensuous delight of beautiful and puissant sound, it continued, to the very end, to thrill. But with a different thrill. It pleased the exacting as much as it satisfied the lovers of "big" and sensuous tone. The magnificent sonorities, the freedom of utterance, the breadth of phrase, the flood of sustained tone, the large vocal intensities endured. It is indeed true that Caruso kept to the end certain vocal idiosyncrasies that made expert listeners grieve and lay hearers rejoice, that he would make his vocal effect even if for the moment he halted the flow or altered the rhythm of the music. Yet the next moment he could shape a phrase, sustain a melody, shade a measure with an exquisite sense of tonal beauty and an equally subtle skill. Moreover, in the quality of that voice as it flooded the theater was a pleasure and an emotion that stirred the common heart of all that heard. There was that, too, in Caruso which commended the man behind. A more honest, a more earnest singer, more willing to do his utmost for his audience and for the opera has never drawn breath. Simple-minded he also was, and his simplicity and his sincerity saved him in operatic impersonation. Admittedly he was no very plausible actor in romantic parts, but when in his honest continence did he offend or amuse the eye? And in his last and mellowed days he was not far from the "grand style" of John of Leyden in "The

Prophet" and Eléazer in "The Jewess." Or give him a homely personage among Italian folk to play and he played him vividly and well. He was, for instance, a believable and amusing comedian in Donizetti's "L'Elisir d'Amore." He characterized the Canio of Leoncavallo's melodrama stirringly and truthfully.

In "Pagliacci" Caruso had a clear notion of his personage that he wrought into a workable and cumulating histrionic design. From year to year, he amplified it with much illuminating and defining detail. Recall, for instance, the exaggerated whimsies of a strolling player with which his matured Canio cozened the crowd at the beginning of the play; the wiping of the powder from his face as of a player resuming relievedly his own person; the intensity, brooding or ominous, that he threw into his declamation in the play while in action he was but doing the part; the fashion in which he went emotionally dead when he had struck down Nedda; how he returned a little to himself, dragged out of his throat "la commedia e finita" and huddled away, distraught, blind, blank again.

Always, too, Caruso's song was the speech of Canio, as elemental in all his moods, as direct and full-voiced in his emotions, as simple or savage as the character really is. He made tellingly but untheatrically the swift change from playful banter over the lightness of women to the amorous and vindictive words about a wife that he already suspects; he did not overdo the celebrated soliloquy as a Canio might utter it; he sang in the final scenes with the accents of the pain and the passion that rend the clown amid the ironies of the make-believe and the reality. The music of Canio suited the best compass and the best quality of his matured voice. Hackneyed, "popular" and all the rest of the damning adjectives of superior righteousness his Canio may have become. But it remained one of the most remarkable operatic impersonations of our time.

VII. Fremstad—Mind and Will

Mme. Fremstad had not been long in opera houses before she discovered that the field of the mezzo-soprano is relatively small. To perceive was to will the gradual quest of a new range, little by little enlarging the compass of her voice and persuading it to new timbres. Her voice ever bore the marks of the strain the transformation had laid upon it, but the change, with all its pains and penalties, was worth the accomplishing. For had she not achieved it our opera houses would have lacked the most illustrious singing-actress of Wagnerian parts since Lehmann and Ternina. Only Mme. Easton has matched her since in the singing of them; no one hereabouts in the acting of them.

By force of penetrating will, by keen and tireless mental energy, by goading pride of achievement, Mme. Fremstad seemed to devise, compose and project most of her impersonations. She was no "temperamental" singing-actress who seized instinctively upon a few elementary emotions and by easy ardor and readiness of means gave them tonal and histrionic life and being. In all her parts, except possibly Venus in "Tannhäuser" and Sieglinde in "Die Walküre," wherein complete, secure and long-standing impersonation hid every means to the illusion, it was possible to discover traces of her processes. Her alert and tireless mind, her resolute imagination searched out of music and text and inner vision the moods and the impulses, the rages and submissions, the raptures and despairs of her Isolde. In its earlier days, her impersonation no more than laid these emotions side by side in flat tints. The illusion of tones and action was as the illusion of an Isolde in clear outline and vivid color in a window of glass.

Then, as Mme. Fremstad ripened the impersonation and herself, these emotions began to appear in the round, to melt their lines into long and sweeping curves of feeling, to fuse their colors into a manifold glow, to animate the whole being of an Isolde who went the way of tragic fate. The voice became as Isolde's at the given moment and in the given stress of the music-drama; the action seemed the spontaneous and inevitable complement. Mme. Fremstad, as Mme. Fremstad, added to it only the expressive richness of her tones and the tragic sweep of her movements. Her impersonation was no longer frescoed upon the stage. It had its being there in the emotional life of music and play. Her threefold Kundry, from its darksome and impenetrable wildness in the first scenes, through its sensuous splendors and subtle suggestion in the garden, to the tranquil beauty of the final episodes underwent a similar evolution. By fine and indomitable will of imagination, she mantled her characterization in mystery, shadowed in the earlier episodes, agonized when Klingsor evokes her magic in the seductions of the garden—they are half-mental and so the better within Mme. Fremstad's powers—and haloed in the transfiguration of the end. No Kundry of the international stage probably matches hers. Only she and Ternina have made head against a perversely baffling part.

Mme. Fremstad's Isolde and Kundry were intricately composed, as Wagner's music and characterization bade. Each was at once a finely and largely wrought vocal and histrionic design sedulously proportioned, colored and shaded. Beside these her Brünnhilde seemed a simpler impersonation, in which one elemental mood or passion gave place to another and each was translated into heroic ardor and sweep of voice and action. Out of a young world came her Valkyr, elate and high-hearted; out of a world already shadowed and out of a spirit deepened, she called Siegmund to Valhalla. The high heart was racked in the parting with Wotan but it kept its pride. Then the exaltation, the desolation, the transfiguration of the two other "Ring" dramas—tragic passion upon tragic passion—that Mme. Fremstad, upborn by the music and by her will, came finally to sustain to the end. There were moments in her Brünnhilde when her voice and action struck swift, heroic fire; there were as many more when her sustained intensity of passionate utterance and passionate pause flooded eye, ear and imagination; and once and again the still magnificence of her repose seemed to fill the stage.

VIII. Coloratura Contrasts—Tetrazzini and Galli-Curci

Mme. Tetrazzini lingers as a very unusual figure on the operatic stage of her day. She is the coloratura singer pure and simple, who sings and does little else besides, of the sort that our fathers and grandfathers were cherishing in the fifties and sixties. Her parts are all old Italian—the mellifluously raving Lucia; Violetta of "Ah! Fors è Lui"; the sorely harried but steadily songful Gilda; Bellini's maiden among Puritans who are singularly expert in the ornaments of song; and the wife in "Crispino" who crowns her conjugal devotion by the brilliant singing of "The Carnival of Venice" or Proch's "Air and Variations." Smilingly through these parts went Mme. Tetrazzini, with matronly amiability and Florentine good nature fairly oozing from her. Not a penny cared her listeners whether to the eye she was not at all like Scott's Lucy Ashton, the Gilda of romantic girlish fancies, or the sleep-walking peasant girl that strays across the quivering bridge in "La Sonnambula." Mme. Tetrazzini, and her auditors as well, heeded not "interpretation." She was there to sing—and sing she did to large and general pleasure, with feats of staccati and trill and swelling and diminishing of the voice—all as though they were the impulse and chance of the moment, when Violetta picks up her train or Gilda climbs the steps to the chamber. Elsewhere Mme. Tetrazzini's voice was less remarkably ordered, but it was, and still remains, the voice of an unusual coloratura soprano.

Succeeding Mme. Tetrazzini in these parts and in public acclamation came Mme. Galli-Curci. Yet with all of the limitations and temptations these "Roman candle operas," as Mary Garden calls them, impose upon a singer, Mme. Galli-Curci does not display herself. She comes out of her personages only to acknowledge the applause at the end of a "scene;" to repeat a few of the glinting measures; to bow casually after applauded "numbers"; while everywhere else she keeps her tones and her action the voice and the bearing of the personage in the circumstances of the opera.

In the "Mad Scene" in "Lucia," as one gently distraught, as one wistfully seeking the betrothed she may not find for the wedding, she comes upon the stage with longing eyes, troubled face, groping gesture. She sings the first measures—the pure song—of the soliloquy in tones so soft, light, clear that they seem to float upon the air; they flow from her lips in edgeless sequence; they are simply colored with the longing that sees but may not grasp—the perfect voice of piteous vision blank to all but what it beholds and desires within itself. Perfection of voice for such music and personage, perfection of artistry in the shaping, the jointure, the curve and the modulation of tone unite to perfect illusion of the character, the instant. Here is Donizetti's music sung as that somewhat pedestrian composer may hardly himself have imagined it.

Mme. Galli-Curci—or rather Lucy Ashton—passes on to "Ardon gl'incensi" and the succeeding ornate measures. With the crystalline sparkle of her staccati, the limpid flow of her runs up or down the scale, the purity and artfulness of her trills in crescendo, the clearness and the brightness of her "skips" (as the old teachers of song named them) over difficult passages, she weaves the pattern of Donizetti's intricate measures. Upon the ear they fall when Mme. Galli-Curci sings them, as upon the eye fall the arabesques above some Moorish doorway in the ruins of Granada when bright Spanish sun shines through them. Yet to that pattern she gives the voice of rhapsody, of the rhapsody that plays childlike, delighted, absorbed with haunting delusions. Again the perfect voice of coloratura singing as the expressive means for which imaginative composers employ it. Everywhere indeed, when Donizetti so embellishes incidentally Lucy's song, Mme. Galli-Curci's voice seems to flower under inner prompting into this ornament. Only one of the feats that she so transmutes into expression of mood or feeling does she seem once and again to use for displayful purposes—her ability to swell a long-held tone—the *mesa di voce* of the old masters.

IX. Titta Ruffo—for Power

As the memoirs, letters and essays have come down to us, the seventeenth and the eighteenth centuries seem more interested in their men-singers than in their women. Half the anthologies of English prose contain Addison's essay about the tenor who slew the lion in the London of Queen Anne. Dr. Burney recounts more of the men that he heard when he wandered through the concert-rooms and the opera houses of Europe than he does of the women. Out of the records of the time it is easy to reconstruct the men that sang in the "original casts" of Mozart's operas in Vienna; but they usually leave the women pale and lifeless shadows. The nineteenth century acclaimed Mario, Jean de Reszké and other tenors, Lablache and other basses, Fauré and a baritone or two; but it was rather the century of the prima donna. When the historians and gossips of music begin to delve among its memorabilia, they are likely to find much more about Malibran and Alboni, Patti and Gerster, Lehmann and Materna than they will about the tenors and the baritones that partnered them on many stages.

In the present century the men seem to have their inning again. With us in America, Caruso became a matter of course from long familiarity with his voice and artistry; but when he made his occasional descents upon Paris, Berlin or Vienna, the public received him as of old it received the primi donne, with no whit less excitement and acclaim. He happened to be a tenor in a time when eminent tenors were few, and it is the good fortune of the high-voiced among men to be sought and extolled above the baritones and basses. They of the lower voices have always been plentiful and capable. From one view their numbers and their ability have been their bane, and they have shone as constellations rather than as individual planets. Besides, as common predilections run, they take "unsympathetic" parts in most operas and while they may impress their hearers mentally, they do not charm them sensuously.

Then, at last, in this operatic age of men-singers, a baritone stirred the same excitement, wonder and mixed admiration as have the primi donne and the primi tenori. Next to Caruso, Titta Ruffo was for some years the most acclaimed man-singer in Europe. In America, at his first appearance, he proved that admiration and excitement over primi donne of both sexes are by no means moribund and are not likely to be unless human nature dies too. Caruso, years ago, made his début in America in routine fashion. New York learned gradually to appreciate Jean de Reszké. Mme. Melba's début in the nineties was a chilly occasion. But Titta Ruffo's was a début comparable in all sorts of excitement—from violent admiration to violent detraction—to Mme. Tetrazzini's.

Mr. Ruffo elected to appear in Hamlet in Ambroise Thomas's opera, so dead and buried that even in Paris, where it was to be resurrected for his centenary, the director of the Opéra had to search for singers who even cursorily knew the parts in it. Mr. Ruffo, it is said, is more ambitious as actor than singer, and so perhaps this phantom of a real Hamlet tempted him. He could hardly have known that Latin Hamlets in opera or drama usually strike Americans as queer. Yet in spite of these handicaps, his acting revealed and maintained two distinctions. It has a singular projecting power and a remarkable command of diction and tonal coloring. There is in him a rare communicative force as out of a strong and vivid personality releasing itself in a similar histrionic temperament. His diction is as puissant, too. It has not the polished elegance of Mr. Zenatello's, for example, but it has an exceeding clearness and it is uncommonly plastic. His transitions from bald declamation to songful phrase are thrilling in their vocal beauty and in their histrionic intensity. The voice that accomplishes these things is a very big voice, still in the noon of its strength, and maintained by the utmost vitality of technical resource. In its highest ranges it has a clear tenor quality. In its middle course, especially when Mr. Ruffo is not propelling it to the full as he is too often wont to do, it has a warm and songful beauty. In its lowest ranges it loses body, distinctive timbre, and becomes an ordinary voice.

What Mr. Ruffo displayed in that first evening in America, he has shown ever since. The great power of tone, the great resources that maintain it, the great power of temperament behind it are at once his glory and his peril. They are his peril when he drives his voice and makes it hard, metallic and merely noisy. They are his peril again when, in the temptation to prolong and intensify telling phrases, they produce unsteadiness of tone. They are his glory when they enable the singer to hold,

III

SINGERS OF SONGS

I. McCormack For All

WHEN a renowned singer of the opera house condescends to the concert-hall, she—for it is oftenest she—usually condescends indeed. Too many of us have heard Miss Farrar rattle a careless voice through a "reel" or two of songs; or Miss Garden variously proving her possession of "personality" to an amused audience; or Mme. Galli-Curci showering high notes prolonged, as so many bonbons upon her hearers. Curiosity and nothing else, these ladies of "the lyric stage" seem to agree, has assembled the listening company. "Play down" to it, they also fondly believe, and let integrity as artist and musician go hang. Thereby, they harvest vogue, fame, money, while from Trenton even to Tulsa mankind and womankind rejoice in them. Yet not one of them excels or equals John McCormack in the enduring favor of the public. Not one has reaped a singer's reward in reputation and riches as he has garnered them. "Any old way" they sing in the concert-hall; while he plies in it every beauty of his voice, every secret of his skill. 'Round and 'round they go in hackneyed, common, showy numbers; while steadily he widens and betters the range of his pieces.

Mr. McCormack is a master of the art of song and therefore still a student of it. He knows the highways and the byways of music, and therefore still explores them that they may yield him new matter. He keeps warm artistic ambition and artistic conscience, sparing no pains of preparation, upbuilding from year to year the quality of his concerts. If he makes occasional sacrifices to his public, from him, as from no other whom it frequents, it has learned many a true quality, many a find standard, of song. If he must prudently yield his hearers their portion of sentimentality, he counters with the rarefied beauty, often high and grave, of his singing of ancient music. Scrutinize one of Mr. McCormack's audiences—and find in it, taking fill of pleasure, not a few connoisseurs of music. It is the custom to call him a "popular singer." He is deservedly. As singing goes in these days, he is also, and quite as often, an aristocrat of song.

Mr. McCormack's program usually begins with a group of eighteenth-century airs. And what other singer of the hour more arduously turns ancient pages, so often shuts the book with treasure in his hands? The impression, the emotion of these songs—from Peri, from Costanza, from Bach, from Mozart, and from the early Händel—is of pure music unadorned. Mr. McCormack can risk the nakedness of such song, his perception grasps its austerities. He can carry it to its heights, understand its breadth, respect its severities. With Händel, too, in his later manner—when the composer chose to lay the ornament of song upon melodic line amply phrased, charged again out of that amplitude with a magnificent melancholy—Mr. McCormack is master. He can summon as by intuition the glow of Händel's "grand manner." The books tell the prowess of ancient singers in this ancient music. Moderns, studious of it, have reason to accept Mr. McCormack as such voice.

To these "old airs" usually succeeds a miscellany of classic French, Russian, German, English pieces. Over all of them plays the familiar beauty of voice—pure tenor still with no reediness to thin it, no baritone darkening to cloud it; the musician's perception, the singer's skill, the imagining and intuitive artist's regard for pace, accent, color; the tone that bears all three, gives

II. Rosing the Russian

Most of us in the Western world heard first of Vladimir Rosing when, exiled from his native Russia, he descended upon English concert-halls. There he won quickly no little note, no small public; while discriminating reviewers, worthy of trust, warmly yet persuasively praised him. Often and with admiration, the major cities of Britain heard him as singer in his own concerts, as "assisting artist" to orchestras, and once and again in opera. Then Mr. Rosing ventured the United States, where, though the reviewers were negligent, stirred audiences heard, applauded and waxed in regard for him. A few, at least, were aware of the coming of an unusual, an engrossing singer, a singer, too, not to be easily compared with any our concert-halls have much known.

Mr. Rosing's voice is a tenor. Heard in stripped song, with neither characterization nor outpoured passion to cloak them, his tones are of clear Italian quality, even as Russian music, in lyrical flow in the opera house, often becomes Italianate.

By this token, Mr. Rosing sings vibrantly, elastically, freely, clearly, yet now and again with a perceptible "whiteness," with play of that plaintive note which in Italian song—and at passing moments with him—easily becomes nasal and wiry. Evidently he is a well schooled and thoroughly practiced singer. When he believes that pure song is voice to the music in hand, he sings with clear regard for well-shaped, transparent tone, sustained line, warm, felicitous Italian phrasing, adept modulation, spun transition, plastic progress, apt climax.

Usually, however, Mr. Rosing prefers to make his song an insistently expressive art. In his tones he would define and project character; summon picture and vision; evoke and convey passions of the mind, the soul, the body. And he would do all these things to the utmost. For such purpose, he bends or breaks rhythms, chops or fuses phrases, zigzags the melodic line, sharply changes pace or accent, emphasizes contrast, multiplies climax. To gain these ends he uses unashamed what the vestal virgins of song call vocal tricks—the falsetto, for example, or the long-sustained note, swelled, diminished, melted almost inaudibly into the air. He uses them, however, not as display in shallow

Galli-Curcian or Tetrazzinian fashion, but to achieve a discoverable point in his vocal design. Above all else, Mr. Rosing would color his tones and impress upon his hearers the personage, the passion, the picture of music and verse as they have stirred his spirit. If the accepted arts of song will so serve him, he uses them expertly, effectively. If they are less viable, he chooses his own means, employs them in his own way. Again out of Russia comes "the new singing." Blessed land, whence always there is something new!

To such pitch has Mr. Rosing carried characterizing purpose and projecting power that the listener forgets the song in the singer. A more "personal" concert than one of Mr. Rosing's is rare indeed. Not even Chaliapin's are more pervaded by a single spirit. He proffers a few words of explanation of his songs, he ventures a happy interchange, Russian-wise, with his audience. He spares neither his own nor the audience's emotion. A score or so of pieces will stand on his programs—folk-songs arranged by various Russian hands; numbers from Musorgsky, Arénsky, Rimsky; from Dargomijsky, Grechaninov, the lesser known Bagrinovsky and Nevstruev. There will be Glinka humorous and sporting in tones with the clicking rhythm of a railway-train; Arénsky in piteous grayness and haunting monotonies; Cui, stark, woeful, delirious; Borodin, satirizing swollen and worldly conceit. With his tones Mr. Rosing pictures—and the listening ear opens the seeing eye as variously—the blank horizons of the endless steppes, the palaces of the great, the cold interior of the peasant's hut. And there is always truth, and also vision, in this tone-picturing.

Again his tones are the voice of passion and then, most of all, he penetrates his hearers with deep illusion. The delirium of a starved peasant crying to his barren lands; the great cry of the heart of a race assembled, multiplied, released—in Grechaninov's invocation to Russia—rise to tragic immensity. Out of himself, as much as from music and verse, Mr. Rosing makes these magnificences. Let the body and the head, flung back almost in contortion, the spoken tone, the sudden gesture, go for the accessory histrionic means they sincerely are. It is the transmitting, the impassioning power of Mr. Rosing that conveys such sensation. There is rhetoric in such singing but an honest, living rhetoric.

III. Culp and Completeness

Julia Culp is unique among the women singers of pure song in this generation. Her artistry is comparable to the artistry which distinguished Mme. Lehmann and Mme. Sembrich, but hers is a closer, a more confining frame. In the interpretation of folk-song, the song of homely sentiment, and in the interpretation of German lieder, she has no peers. The songs, in particular, of Schubert and Brahms naturally invite her—Schubert, perhaps, by the lyric sensibility and the artful modulation of melody, to both of which her tones and talents are as sensitive as a mirror; Brahms, in turn, by the large sweep, the deepening and darkening coloring, the moody intensity of not a few of the pieces that she usually chooses from him. In the sonorities and the sustaining power of her tones, in her own cast of mind and imagination, is that which answers richly to his matter and manner.

But whoever the composer, where he ends she begins—in the tone-picturing and wistful longing of Schubert's song of Suleika, for instance; in the piteous and darksome passion that swells out of his "Mädchen's Klage"; in the homely directness of feeling and imagery, the universality of humble emotion, elate or sorrowing, that makes the songs of Franz perennially touch the hearts of human kind; in the light fancies or the graver moods of Cornelius; in the folk-song note that Brahms could strike in his songs of the loveliness of German landscapes, of the luring coquetry of amorous German girls, of rude and energetic German men-folk. There is that in the mind and imagination of such composers as Schubert, Brahms, Wolf and Franz that they may not set down upon music-paper though they stretch notes and directing words to the utmost. For they can do no more than seek to enkindle the singer and leave the passion, the poetry, the vision, the scene that engrossed and fired them to her answering imagination. Not once in vain do they ask of Mme. Culp such fulfillment. And when the balladry of England or Scotland, France or America find place on her programs, Mme. Culp is also intuitive interpreter. Folk-song it is the custom to call them. Yet some one must originally have made them, sung them. What he imagined and set in his notes, Mme. Culp fulfills in her tones and her hearers know the richness of simplicity. For folk-pieces, even "arranged," ought to sound as though the singer were recalling them or inventing them for the first time. When Mme. Culp sings them, they do.

There is no word but splendor for the voice of Mme. Culp. Her lower notes have their soberly glowing depths; her middle notes their luscious and opulent fullness; her high notes their radiant and expansive warmth. Her half-voice is of velvety texture; her softest tones spin the gossamer filaments of beautiful sound; her amplest notes gain its richest resonance. And always those notes, however changeful, proceed in unbroken flow. Phrase melts into phrase with no more outward sign of jointure than have wavelets in the water; modulation seems as impulse, yet unerring. And meanwhile upon her song in such voice and so ordered, she bestows all the glories of color that insight, intuition and imagination, analysis and synthesis may yield. Again there is no word but splendor for the vitalizing, the revealing, the transmitting quality of Mme. Culp's song. She harvests the poet; she garners the composer; she enriches both.

IV. GERHARDT—GERMAN-SCHOOLED

Another singer of German lieder less impeccable and with clearer limitations than Mme. Culp, is Elena Gerhardt. Her voice is most pleasurable in its middle tones. With them her technical skill is most secure and adroit; while they have more variety of force and color and more expressive quality than any other part of her voice. She is mistress of sustained feeling, rapturous, pictorial, homely. She sings, for example, "Weyla's Song," out of Hugo Wolf, a glowing picture of an enchanted island—such an island as rises in Boecklin's pictures—and the glow of intense longing is in her tones. In another vein goes the "Brauner Bursche" of Brahms's gypsy songs—the gay vein of the youth dancing the Czardas with his sweetheart, and flinging down his money exultantly, showily. She excels, then, in the impartment of a single mood, picture or emotion in sustained song and within the frame she is capable of much variety of expression.

So, too, she excels in the songs of robust, resolute, hearty, homely emotion dear to German composers and German audiences. Such a song is Brahms's "The Smith," her beloved encore piece. Akin is Schumann's "Ins Freie," which she sings with ringing and reiterated declamatory intensity. She is expert, too, in the lighter vein of this homeliness. Where she falls short on the side of imagination and expression is in songs that are half narrative, half characterization—and to add a third half, Irish-wise—half picture. Her tones are not as graphic as they might be, for instance, in Schumann's song of the girl telling her whimsical fortune at cards, and they do not quite bring the moodiness of Liszt's song of the three gypsies and of the philosophizing bystander. She accomplishes such pieces with perceiving and practised intelligence, but she is able singer achieving the song, and not as she sometimes is, the perfectly attuned instrument to it.

Yet, whatever Miss Gerhardt's details, she differentiates the music of the five signal composers of German song—Schumann, Brahms, Liszt, Strauss and Hugo Wolf—and so makes keen pleasure in the concert hall. She catches the rapturous glow of Schumann's romantic music and the voice of romance is in his songs as in no other. She does

V. For Voice, Hempel

Frieda Hempel's hearers have equal reason to applaud her in the concert-hall or in the opera house. At last she is as gratefully heard in a recital of songs as she was as singer of lyric music from the tentative days of her Violetta in "Traviata" to the crowning evening of her finely tempered and rounded Princess in "Der Rosenkavalier." Slowly she has learned the evasive art of program-making. Once and again in the past her choice of pieces has been irritation to her more cultivated and exacting hearers. Now she compliments equally the taste and intelligence of singer and listeners.

The quickest, easiest, the most salient pleasure of Miss Hempel's song is the pleasure of a voice in its golden prime. Elderly singers too long haunt the stage and let the memories of their better days work indulgence for them. Younger singers come too hastily upon it, and the promise of their future, if only they will take the time and spare not with the toil, persuades the listener to overlook the shortcomings of a careless eagerness and confidence. Singers of no particular age let "personality," intelligence, imagination veil vocal limitations that, removed, would make the other qualities shine only the brighter. Vocally, on the other hand, Miss Hempel asks no indulgences, proffers no excuses —and needs none. Her rich soprano tones flow warmly, in full body; they are even and edgeless through the whole range of a voice of no small compass; they are supple to her will as it plays upon the contours, the contents, the colors of the music; they are crystalline in depth and transparency; they give off glowing lusters.

Miss Hempel's voice unmistakably recalls Mme. Melba's in her noon, mistrustful as that elder generation will be which likes to believe that there can be no younger singers like the singers it knew. Miss Hempel's tones are comparable with Mme. Melba's in union of lustrous softness with clear brilliance, of sumptuous body with exceeding agility, of lyric sweetness with florid sparkle, in a silvery quality that captures the ear while it evades words. The kinship recurs, again, when out of stores of breath and with wondrous evenness, Miss Hempel sustains her upper tones through the long rapturous phrases of the melody that is one unbroken skyward winging, in Händel's air from "Atalanta;" when the ear knows not whether to admire more the lyric loveliness of the middle and purely songful strophe of "Casta Diva" or the showering fioriture of the end; when a "vocal waltz" swirls in a glittering spray of the ornaments of song, but never loses rhythmic flow while modulation becomes as playful ripple. Yet not even Mme. Melba herself could have declaimed the recitative that prefaces "Casta Diva" with such opulence of phrase and such propulsive power as Miss Hempel gives to it in perfect blend of lyric and dramatic singing. Upon trifles, too, Miss Hempel not only bestows the glamors of her voice but also the instinct of the comédienne in tones. In Beethoven's ditty about Chloë and her kiss, Miss Hempel brings such archness as Mme. Sembrich used to bring to light lyrics and that Miss Hempel may have learned in her studies with that mistress of song.

VI. Destinn, Violin-Like

As there is no word but splendor for the singing of Mme. Culp there is no word but beauty for the singing of Emmy Destinn in the few ripe years before she withdrew from public appearance. There were beauty of voice, beauty of artistry, beauty of insight and impression, beauty even in the presence of the singer herself aglow with the penetrating and quickening charm that is the birthright of these fine-fibred Czech women. The happy analogue of Miss Destinn's voice in song is the tone that Mr. Kreisler draws from the violin. It had a like soft, lustrous and finely spun texture; it moved in a delicately vibrant progress from undulation into undulation; it was as full of adroit and iridescent shadings; it had the same soft clear warmth and exquisite sensibility; it was controlled by the same fine artistry penetrating the hearer until it transported him into a world in which there is naught else for the moment but the possessing loveliness of sound.

Of like beauty was the artistry of Miss Destinn's singing when the ear set to the close watching and the mind to the close analyzing of it—all delicate poise and intuitive and astute finesse, all sure and bright little strokes that blended like the pointillage of an impressionistic picture into a perfectly designed and illusory whole. And this whole was the pervasive speech of the music, of the personage who is singing it—if the piece happened to be an operatic number—of the emotions in play over it, of Miss Destinn, responsive and enkindled thereby in voice, in imagination, in her whole embodying and transmitting being.

Recall Miss Destinn's singing of the air of the young Salome enamored of the Baptist in Massenet's "Hérodiade," and the recalling is to hear anew the soft and insinuating timbre of her caressing tones. Hers was the very rustle of the sensual impulses that Massenet sought in his music. Yet the sheer beauty of the singer's tones and feeling idealized them. Recall, again, her singing of her native music, from Dvoràk, in particular. Out of it rose the penetrating and haunting beauty, the native wildness and wistfulness, the whole exotic color of Czech song. Again, the analogue is Mr. Kreisler. For it is his crowning virtue, as it was Miss Destinn's, to make the ab-

VII. Teyte via Paris

Maggie Teyte came to America with one of the "testimonials" that Debussy used occasionally to emit, to sing his songs and the songs of other contemporary French composers. She had dwelt in Paris in the inmost circles of the "new school" and was said there to have imbibed the "only true and authentic" versions of its songs. Then, and since then, no one has sung them so well or so characteristically. Her voice is a rather singular one, a distinctly French voice, English-born though she is. There is a faint nasal quality in it, a hint of dryness akin to that which makes most French tenors sing like sublimated baritones. Sometimes, too, a tone in it has a very fine but still perceptible edge. It is a very bright voice that has been polished into a kind of dry clearness. It does lack richness; it does lack sensuous warmth. It falls on the ear much as the light of a very clear, dry, cool, still autumn day falls on the eye. There are glints in Miss Teyte's tones; they are transparent, prismatic, catching many reflections from the music and the mood of the songs that she sings. Italians would not like her voice; they would say it lacked sensuous richness. The English would believe they ought to like it, because it is a voice for connoisseurs. The French warm to it—because it is so French a voice in all its distinctive traits. We Americans may take it as individuals. Perhaps it is fairest to say that the mind as well as the ear appreciates it—the instrument is so polished, so limpid, so serviceable to its purpose.

Miss Teyte can run the Debussyan gamut. For the first time we in America heard Debussy humorous—in the song of the bourgeoisie and their Sunday "excursions." For the first time, too, we heard Debussy half-sensual, half-melancholy in the song of Bilitis's tresses. Besides there was Debussy playful and mocking, in the song of the puppets; ghostly again in the phantoms of the moonlight; finding in the sea and its colors and sounds strange images of stuffs and their hues and rustlings; Debussy languorously ecstatic, Debussy bitter-sweet; and always Debussy subduing the images of lights and sounds and colors to the melancholy they stirred in the soul they touched. Therein is the poetic formula of the new French song. It is as characteristic and sometimes as arbitrary as the harmonies. Usually Miss Teyte's transparent tones are full of the reflections of all these images. Sometimes a single phrase in them makes an emotion, a fancy, glint. It is altogether sensitive, polished and calculating singing. It etches out Debussy's songs. Yet some of us may like them better when they are as vague as a Monet or as richly sensuous of color as a Renoir.

VIII. Gauthier the Pioneer

To the living composers of song, after Debussy, Eva Gauthier gives voice. Her artistry, like the artistry of Miss Teyte, although it achieves different ends, is the artistry of sophistication. As signal interpreter of the moderns and ultra-moderns she is to song what Miss Garden is to opera. She is mistress of tonal imagery and tonal illusion.

An audience which assembles to hear Miss Gauthier is a pleasure in itself. It usually wears bright clothes, for it is a cheerful company come for pleasure and not from a sense of duty or in semi-boredom. It includes many young listeners, come to hear and to applaud youth. The singer herself usually meets more than halfway the mood of the audience. Her gown shines with color, while a touch of fantasy has shaped it. She diffuses a hint of the exotic, as though face and hair had caught lasting imprint of her Javanese days. She also comes eagerly, alertly, to her task and is quick to reciprocate the pleasure of her audience.

Hers is the thoroughbred instinct to be always doing her best.

To this personal quality, which is not exactly the routine of the concert-hall. Miss Gauthier may owe her audiences. Yet her choice of pieces, her unique place among present singers in America, help to swell them. Usually her programs are plentiful in music of this immediate day. For her, indeed, none of it may be too venturesome or too baffling. With it she oftens fills an entire concert, letting the new men, the bold men, of France, Italy, England, Germany and America, wreak for two hours what detractors call their wicked or their foolish way. She sings fantastical songs out of Stravinsky; ironic pieces out of the Parisians, Ravel and Satie; the newest numbers of Malipiero and Casella, the "advanced" Italians—in fine, a wholly exceptional and altogether singular music to be heard in America from no one else in such understanding and sympathy. She summons and sustains the atmosphere in which each song has its being and out of herself animates, intensifies and colors it. At her command is the mood, the passion, the picture of every song; while, again out of herself she shades, warms and deepens them. Into her singing passes every inflection, every suggestion of the composer, be it a golden image of Duparc, a sensuous tremor of Debussy, an ironic stroke of Ravel. Often she matches subtlety for subtlety, producing the "sounds" of the new music, achieving no less its direct, pungent, instant impression, its brevities, its recurring harshness, its smart and smack. And throughout this multifold accent and coloring her voice keeps often to the beauty and obeys not a few of the prescriptions of pure song. So in her and for a pleasure that set her hearers aglow, two artistries join hands.

IX. Schumann-Heink and Service

When a singer stands at maturity the passing years do not ripen the voice, but they do refine and deepen artistry. Not so many years ago Mme. Schumann-Heink's singing was large outpouring of floods of rich tone, broadly colored with elementary moods and impulses, direct in its musical and emotional appeal, conquering by the intensity of its power and the opulence of its beauty. The voice as mere voice has now lost something of its tonal magnificence. For bursts of tone she now substitutes adroit light and shade in the coloring of it. Great sweeps of power give way to a quieter, deeper, more sustained beauty. To the impulses of a big and warm temperament succeed the finer strokes of thoughtful and ripened imagination.

Mme. Schumann-Heink still keeps the humanness of aspect and voice, mood and emotion, the suggestion of the common lot glorified and ennobled in her, that make her the most sympathetic and the most democratic singer of these days in America. The common people—to use a convenient but not a deprecatory phrase—rejoice in her. She stirs them because her singing expresses in terms that they can feel and understand, moods and emotions that are half-inarticulate in them, and because it awakens spontaneously their half-dormant sense of beautiful and moving song. At the same time, the voice and the artistry that she plies upon it are the pleasure of the sophisticated and the sensitive. In her time, consciously or unconsciously, she has done great service to the broader understanding and appreciation of the art of song in America. She has spread broadcast its satisfactions and pleasures, opened them to a great half-deaf and half-dumb world that scarcely guessed them.

Those that still crave the old Schumann-Heink of the big sweep may still have it when she chooses to place on her programs fragments from the operas of her prime, her somewhat melodramatic version of "The Erl-King" or, less deservingly, the plaint of Rachel crying with the voice of distraught motherhood for her children. Yet even they must feel what a far finer thing is the rich, warm, velvety beauty of her sustained song, falling on the ear like the pile of a thick, soft carpet to the naked foot; the depths of subdued yet glowing color that she may still give it—colors like those in Venetian pictures; and the imagination that catches and weaves each phrase into the spirit of the whole. Once Mme. Schumann-Heink sang with a careless opulence of power. Now when she chooses, she sings with a discriminating artistry, and so gilds and glamors her song. At twilight, in her still ripens the triple resource of the great singer—voice, artistry and life.

IV

PIANISTS

I. Paderewski—Poetry and Power

WHAT was it that differentiated Paderewski from the other pianists of a past and an immediate generation? When he was minded to exercise all his powers that the music in hand asked and when they answered readily to his call, he was distinctly different from his fellows, however eminent. The contrast depended only slightly upon external circumstance. It did not lie in the fact that Paderewski preferred that the lights be lowered while he was playing and so, as some like to believe, clothed music and performance in atmosphere—if only it would come by so easy a trick!—whereas Mr. Bauer or Mr. Gabrilowitsch sit at the piano in full day. It did not come from the fact that Paderewski is a man of courtly and somewhat old-fashioned manners and of like individual habit in his dress whereas Mr. Hofmann or Mr. Godowsky is as routine toward his audience as he is to the eye. It did not even proceed from the fact, commonly said to indicate a greatness apart, that Paderewski could be as inconsiderate toward his hearers—say in promptness and in the temperature of the concert-room—as he was courteous to them in other things. Only in relatively little did it spring from the fact that he was and is interesting and impressive to see, whereas nearly all the pianists of the first rank in this day seem to the sight but ordinary men of an ordinary world, busy with the practice of their profession.

It is an old surmise and probably a true one that many have gone to hear Paderewski to whom music is an unpleasant noise and a piano only a keyed and wired box that makes it. The presumption is that they sought the concert because they had reason to believe that Paderewski was an unusual and impressive personality and that they stayed to the end because on that score he interested and stimulated them. Mr. Bauer, Mr. Gabrilowitsch, even Mr. Busoni, do not seize the eye of the body and the eye of the imagination when they cross the stage to the piano or hold them fast, while they are playing. Paderewski did. In the tall, spare and slightly bent figure; in the leonine and aureoled head; in the deep-set eyes; in the powerful yet sensitive hands; in the air of quiet concentration and courteous detachment there was that which suggested an unusual and an impressive personality. As Paderewski played—no matter through what range of pieces and no matter whether he was at his fullest and highest or a degree or two below them—the impression deepened and, before the concert was done, the listener, even if he was none too quick-minded, felt that he was in the presence of a great and a unique figure. He may not have known that Paderewski was and is scholarly and lettered, a man of many interests in and out of the arts, a man of the world in any company however disposed; and even a man of business of appreciable acumen. He may never have surmised that the pianist was so manifold that he would have risen high in almost any other calling, as indeed he did through his late excursions into European diplomacy and Polish politics. But that same listener unmistakably felt the personal quality and force of the man. None other of the pianists of the day yields such sensation. To the eyes and the sensibilities of their hearers they are only uncommonly able and interesting practitioners of an art.

Therein, at bottom, the difference lies, when the practiced and discriminating listener scrutinizes the qualities of Paderewski as pianist and musician. Mr. Gabrilowitsch plays Schumann's "Carneval" and his listeners hear with pleasure the graphic, fanciful and often poetized panorama in tones that he unrolls before them. Mr. Busoni has made Bach's music magnificently eloquent of substance, form and creative passion. Mr. Hofmann penetrates Beethoven's later sonatas with lucid insight and deep understanding; he imparts them with grave power. In twenty pieces, it is possible to recall the perceiving imagination and the imparting ardor with which Harold Bauer renews their beauty and reanimates their force, and so onward with one and another pianist of the first rank. Hearing, the listener admires the wealth, the plasticity and the readiness of technical resource and verve that they bring to the music; their clear mental, emotional and spiritual response to it; the diverse eloquence with which they impart matter and manner, mood and suggestion; their sense of style; their feeling for color; their poetizing impulses; their play of answering emotion, and so forth with a score of admirable and exalted attributes. But always on the stage is the virtuoso and in the auditorium the hearer, each discharging his due function.

Relatively seldom does any one of these illustrious pianists transport his audience—lifting it out of itself, making it unaware of means and unconscious of process, flooding it with the music that he is playing and with the power of his own projecting and suffusing personality, immersing it in the single and overmastering sensation of the beauty, the passion and the poetry of sound that imagination and exaltation have made music. Often, when he was in full possession of every faculty and deeply stirred by his music Paderewski could so transport his audience. To do so is the achievement of a unique, manifold, almost epical power. For a while this power seemed to wane in the concert-hall because for the time he chose to divert it to the study-table. There he sought to compose music—piano pieces in the larger forms, a symphony, an opera—even as he played it. The attempt and the outcome must have disclosed to his clear mind, as it did to many another not so clear, that only in the interpreting and the imparting of the music of other men could he fully release himself and sweep his hearers into the world of tonal passion and poetry, tonal vision and tonal pageant, that seemed to surge upon his imagination. He returned again to the concert-hall after this experiment and could still use that imagination undiminished, even heightened, with like transporting outcome.

But Paderewski was much more than a pianist clothed with power and passion. For another of the distinctions that to the day of his retirement set him apart from other pianists, was the range and evenness of his technical and interpretative, his pianistic, his musical and his poetizing faculties. There is reason to praise Mr. Busoni for his mastery of technical intricacies and his grave eloquence; Mr. Hofmann for his loveliness and variety of tonal color, for his lucidity, for his manly continence; Mr. Gabrilowitsch for an exceeding beauty of touch and tone and for a temperament that knows both power and charm; Mr. Bauer for a rare limpidity and surety of technical means and for a finely discriminating sense of styles. And so on through the list. In contrast Paderewski assembled in himself and exercised of himself—in greater or less but always in high degree—nearly all the resources and all the qualities of an Olympian pianist.

II. Gabrilowitsch and Bauer—Compeers

Mr. Gabrilowitsch and Mr. Bauer are musicians before they are virtuosi. As pianists they would both cultivate their calling in all its range. Even in these days when each is in the fullness of his power and vogue, they are as ready as ever to bear their parts in chamber-music, to play concertos in which the piano is hardly more than an instrument added to the orchestra. Mr. Gabrilowitsch will even divide his energies as established conductor of the Detroit Symphony Orchestra and as occasional pianist in recitals of his own. It is easy to associate their playing. It is an old story that in both of them mind and feeling as they play upon music are as wide and supple in range as they are even and poised in application. They are the "intimate" pianists, as the youngsters like to say, who bid sympathetic hearers to their confidence.

Mr. Gabrilowitsch came first to America an interesting and expert pianist. He has now become a distinguished pianist in the ripeness of maturity. The sonorous, sweeping, declamatory Gabrilowitsch of Tschaikovsky's concerto is almost at another pole from the Gabrilowitsch gently weaving Mozart's elegant arabesques, singing with Schubert's free-voiced music or meditative over the pieces of Brahms's twilight years. When a pianist can so differentiate his playing, there is no doubting his technical artistry; when he is so sensitive to the particular quality of his several pieces, there is no mistrusting his response to the emotion and the poetry of music; and when he accomplishes this discrimination as justly as Mr. Gabrilowitsch, there is no mistaking the poise and controlling intelligence behind. Thus does he stand in the possession of the three attributes of a pianist in the high, full sense of the word—mental grasp of his music and mental control of his playing, susceptibility to the peculiar beauty and the particular emotion or mood of his pieces, and the executive ability to bring his understanding of them and his feeling for them to clear and persuasive expression.

In the concert-room Mr. Gabrilowitsch, in himself, lacks the immediate appeal of an unusual personality. He escapes, indeed, the pedagogic air of Mr. Bauer, the businesslike routine of Mr. Hofmann or the somnolent heaviness of Mr. Lhévinne.

He lacks equally the quick sense of alert power that sprang from Mme. Carreño, for example, as she crossed the stage to the piano; the impression of an uncanny and impish personality that de Pachmann bore through the very door of the anteroom, or the suggestion of mingled remoteness and power that was in Paderewski's presence. When Mr. Gabrilowitsch has gone half his way through a recital, it is easy to find in his bearing the poise, the tensity, the alertness, the token of a finely-tempered mind and spirit that are in his playing. He looks his absorption in it, he suggests his elastic control of himself and all that he would do. The sense of personality, however, is neither uppermost in the hearer as it was with de Pachmann nor electric and almost compulsory as it was with Paderewski. A departing audience recalls Mr. Gabrilowitsch the man less than Mr. Gabrilowitsch the pianist. Advance as he may, he is never likely to have the reward—perhaps experience is the truer word—of clamorous women close packed about his platform. Yet he will leave his listeners as he leaves them now, with haunting memories of his playing. He stirs, and, in all probability, will stir to the end, not to loud enthusiasm, but to intent and intimate admiration.

It is within the truth to call Mr. Gabrilowitsch and Mr. Bauer objective pianists, to say, even, that they have gone to extremes in self-subjection. It were fairer and truer to call them poised pianists. No one who has heard them often and widely can doubt either the large amplitude or the nervous vigor of their power when the music demands it. Deliberate and polished as they can be, they can be equally free and spontaneous. The truth is that being no virtuosi with a technique and a temperament and little else, but men of fine mind and practiced intelligence, they discriminate with their music. They find as nearly as they can the particular characteristics of each piece, and set themselves to the imparting. To the end they are likely to remain the intimate pianists, seeming, indeed, oftenest to be playing to themselves, while by some happy chance their audience has been admitted to hear, and they are hardly aware of its presence.

Mr. Gabrilowitsch, in particular, is plainly conscious, thoughtful even, of the ends that he would gain, but these ends are the perfect impartment of the music in its kind, and not the glory of Ossip Gabrilowitsch or the answering excitement of the audience. He may or may not have stirred or pleased it, but once more he has brought the music to life—the daily re-creation which is the marvel of the pianist's or the violinist's existence—as it lives in him.

Mr. Bauer's studious mind searches deeply, minutely, persistently into each composer whose music he plays, into each piece that he finally harvests for performance in public. He likes to turn aside from the beaten track and out of the byways fetch an overlooked or a semi-archaic piece. His inquiring mind will not let him believe that the "standard repertory" contains all things that a pianist should play or that a properly curious audience cares to hear. Having so chosen his music, strange or familiar, he bestows upon it a mind that assorts, defines and rounds, a temperament as clear and just, technical resource that gains his every purpose. With Mr. Bauer, from the abstruse concertos of Brahms to the evanescent fancies of Debussy, the listener hears the music integral and illuminated, of, by and for itself.

III. Rakhmaninov the Puritan

Like Paderewski, but in less degree, Mr. Rakhmaninov is possessed of a personality which arrests his audience—an audience, too, which in diversity sometimes recalls his predecessor. But to this audience Mr. Rakhmaninov plays in his own fashion. He does not caress his hearers with an insinuating beauty, an illuding glamour of tone; rather, at moments his touch is appreciably metallic, a little thin, perilously brittle. No more does he invariably persuade his hearers that the piano is an instrument of unfolding song. Quite as often with him it is an instrument that parts phrase from phrase, even note from note. As little, is Mr. Rakhmaninov displayful technician. True, there is hardly a pianistic feat of strength or agility (to use the phrase of the circus posters) that he cannot accomplish easily. But he does each and all of these feats as though they were the merest convolutions of the music, or decorations upon it. They are; therefore why stress them?

No more is Mr. Rakhmaninov the poetizing

pianist, transmuting each piece with his own awakened imagination, like Paderewski. He has personality and to spare; but he is not a very "personal" pianist. He is all for the music in hand, to release and enhance the composer's design—and not the pianist's. Evenly and exactly, coolly and detachedly, he does what the composer bids. Flawless master of every technical device, this prowess never labors, never intrudes itself. It accomplishes all things technical for what they are —precisely. The voice of this prowess is a tone as clear—and often as cool—as a crystal. It is a transparent mirror of the music to the uttermost detail; it reflects as completely and lucidly the mood in which the pianist is imparting it. At his will and hands, this tone runs a gamut of gradations as exact as they are endless. It moves in masses and it moves in filaments; it gathers force and it droops to whisper. Chameleon-like, it assumes on the instant whatever color the pianist would impose. Like the technical prowess, this touch and tone is Mr. Rakhmaninov's precise, poised and perfect medium. In both, mind and hand, continence and cultivation are in impeccable mingling. A Puritan comes among pianists.

By these means Mr. Rakhmaninov sets forth the design, the course, the structure of the music in hand. He misses neither the large lines nor the interwoven detail; no modulation, no ornament may escape his clear eyes, his adjusting fingers. The songful unfolding of a melody, the play and interplay of motives or fragments of motives, the beat of rhythm changeful or sustained, the tonal progress, however intricate, the tonal design however obscure, contrast, climax, the levels and the slopes between—not so much as one evades him. Revelation of the form, the substance, the purely tonal content of the composer's measure, is as precise, flawless, complete as the other virtues.

Yet composers also infuse into their music picture, poetry, passion, fervors, fantasy—all the works—at their will and mood—of the imagination, flickering inward or quivering outward. Thoughtfully, assiduously, exactly, Mr. Rakhmaninov photographs these things upon the sensitive plate of his mind. In like manner his touch and tone convey the picture, as the print is to the negative. He "interprets" (as the word goes) with every virtue of musical photography; but with such photography he is done. The portrait, the landscape, the fresco, the miniature, fused and heated with the blended imaginations and individualities of composer and interpreter, he cannot and he will not paint. Again the Puritan of pianists by Puritans applauded.

IV. The Gamut of Tone—Hofmann

Josef Hofmann matured late, but he matured magnificently. In him now are all the qualities of a great pianist as they have not mingled in any single man since the golden prime of Paderewski. He is not a "personality" in the concert-hall; he is even a prosaic figure there. But he happens to be a great musician and a very great pianist, and by these two attributes he can hold the interest of his hearers, however miscellaneous his audience, responsive to the end of a recital. No longer, in his present estate, can he be called the "pianists' pianist." If once he was austere, exact, he has now waxed with emotional, imaginative, characterizing, dramatizing power. And more, he has infused into his playing a new sense of beauty; while out of it, at due moments, springs the quality that he has hitherto lacked—poetic charm.

The glory of Mr. Hofmann, as of Mr. Kreisler, is his wealth and individuality of tone animating and transfiguring the music he plays. No pianist of our time summons a tone so lustrous as that of Mr. Hofmann, so like a crystal through which flow a hundred tints and shadings of tint. Sensitiveness to color and luminosity are its twofold distinctions. It can be richly clangorous as at moments in Schumann's Fantasia or in Liszt's Rhapsodies. It can be so fleet, light, elastic and glinting that the stars shall seem to dance in it through the Waltzes of Chopin. It can be also an exquisitely soft and limpid tone—a tone that distills phrases out of the air into beauty—as with Schumann's "Bird as Prophet." It can spin threads of arabesques as though they were interlacing filaments of color weaving themselves around the song that it also is bearing to as many-hued beauty. Mr. Hofmann's tone is like the voice of a superlative singer in the sensuous beauty that it evokes from the instrument that, as some say, is least dowered with it. Therein is his power—and to much greater degree than when he elects to make the piano sonorous—and therein is the play of his imagination and feeling. The sensations that his music awakes in him are the sensations of the range, the beauty and the power of tones. Grave as he is, "mental" as he is, he plays to the senses of those that hear.

V. Busoni for Bach

In Europe, Mr. Busoni is composer, manifold musician, teacher of and theorist about music. To us in America, he continues a wandering and unique virtuoso. The more the pity, since he is a highly individualized, variously interesting and altogether remarkable figure in the music of our time. There was not, and is not, one that matches him in the music of Bach, whether he plays it as the composer put it on paper or in his own transcriptions, giving to its substance and spirit the richer resource of modern tonal speech. Many a pianist sets them on his programs and plays them after his kind; but there is none that plays them as does Busoni himself.

Mr. Busoni, in his American days, was not of romantic mind and temper and, wisely enough, he was chary of the music of Chopin. He might well also have put aside the piano-pieces of Schumann and Schubert. He seemed to play such numbers with sheer power of mental grasp upon them rather than with imagination and intuition. Music of large and deep matter stirred him but the intimate music of fleeting fancies and poetized and visionary musings more evaded him. For him the large and lofty utterance.

But the very qualities of mind and temperament that parted him from Schumann and Chopin brought him close to Bach's preludes and fugues and to the later sonatas of Beethoven. He played the preludes in sonorities that even upon the piano were organ-like in their depth and richness. The music advanced in majestic clangors; each phrase had its just emphasis; the whole moved with might and majesty. It was truly of the rare and usually impossible grandeurs of the piano. The fugues he swept rushingly and even fantastically forward. They came from his hands like a magnificent improvisation of enkindled mind and spirit of which technical accomplishment was the practiced and instinctive servant. And when the music demanded, he could be gay and humorsome. Eloquent as he could be with the play of arabesque over sustained melody and in the blending and contrasting of voices he could, when he chose, be as light, as playful, as adept as Bach often was in these, his tonal sports and pastimes. In them—and surprisingly—he could charm as, in more sonorous moment, he could thrill.

VI. Moiseiwitsch and Intellect

We are at the turn, as it were, in the passage of pianists. In the newer generation, qualities of the mind expressing themselves in reciprocal qualities of the hand are uppermost in Mr. Hofmann, in Mr. Bauer, in measure in Mr. Gabrilowitsch, in germ in Mr. Levitski. They hark back to Busoni—penetrating and individual intellect, measuring imagery, sentiment and emotion—rather than to Paderewski, passionate and poetic spirit releasing itself in tones.

Of this intellectual line is Benno Moiseiwitsch. His mind discovers and adjusts the design of the composer in the piece in hand; chooses and sets in proportionate array the technical resources whereby he may compass it. By exercise of the intellect rather than by spontaneous play of responsive temperament, Mr. Moiseiwitsch seems to apprehend and distill the particular beauty of voice or mood that the composer would evoke; the emotion, sentiment, picture, vision that has brought the piece into being. By similar transfer from one mind to another the creative faculty in the composer becomes the re-creative faculty in the pianist.

Then to the technical means. Again they are the exercises of a penetrating, precise, perfecting mind. Mr. Moiseiwitsch's tone is richly sonorous without trace of roughness, coarseness, overstrain. It is luminous without a hint of the hardness of an overcrystalline touch. It is endlessly supple; yet not an outline is blurred. Of many colors, of many accents, yet always in adept proportion is this tone. It achieves both beauty and power. It is a tone admirably suited to the music of Brahms whose endless and intricate technical exactions he can sweep before him, whose grave, moody and sometimes abstruse wanderings he can play with an impression of continuous creative and re-creative fire. With many of the modern composers, too, he is in intellectual accord. He is clearly of kin to Ravel, for instance, whose piece of the fountains and the water-god he makes a little marvel of tonal illusion and graphic imagery. There is mystery and magic, too, in his interpretations of Debussy. He can compass the bright, crisp or broken rhythms of Cyril Scott. His is a tone lacking only the sensuous loveliness which up-springs from a mind and spirit softer in fiber; the emotional thrill that is born of a temperament in which there is less reflection and more instinct. This lack denies him the finest romantic sensibility, the freest of romantic zest. His Chopin, for instance, may gain a songful or brooding or visionary beauty. But here and there are a slowness of pace at which it is possible to demur, an almost too precise articulation, without sufficient poetizing affluence.

VII. Novaes Newly Risen

Miss Novaes continues, for the younger generation of pianists, the great line. Youth, comeliness and unobtrusive absorption in her task that seems to leave no room for thought of an audience, commend her. As technician, she is finely apt rather than energetic, or what the commonplaces of the concert-hall call "brilliant." That is to say in such show-pieces as Liszt's "Forest-Murmurs," "Dance of Gnomes" and Rhapsodies, the ear notes the limpidity of her scales, the brightness of her trills, the flowing grace of her arpeggii, the evenness of her runs, the roundness of her octaves, rather than the practiced, ready skill so accomplishing them. Not one touch has she, but many—to distribute the coloring of her tone from mellow glow through sustained radiance to airy sparkle. A tone so sensitive and poised to clearness, force, hue, is sure betokening of a keenness of intelligence, a ripeness of temperament, rare in so young a pianist. Already—and for further marvel—Miss Novaes appreciates both the limitations and the possibilities of her instrument. Not once does she try to force it to quasi-thunderous voice, to stretch it to quasi-orchestral range of timbre and color. Yet at every turn she summons its more songful speech and utilizes the diversities and contrasts of tonal color that it may yield. Her sense of design with the music, of proportion with the piano, also applauds her. Never does she let pianistic fancy harden into mere pianistic display. As an imaginative musician writes, so an imaginative musician plays. Beyond peradventure an old head sits upon her young shoulders.

Miss Novaes, in her present estate, is doubly fortunate. She is not to be taken for granted and she is remembered. On the way to a concert by Mr. Hofmann, Mr. Bauer, Mr. Grainger, even by the young Mr. Levitzki, the listener knows in measure what to expect; at the concert itself, with rare exception for better or for worse, he usually receives it. The "following" of every pianist would have him so; it is our American way to set and fix every artist in his appropriate niche. Perish his audiences, if he happens to be restless there. Miss Novaes is still comparative newcomer; freshly ears await her; while she herself at each hearing amplifies powers, enriches pleasure.

Thereby she is clearly remembered, anticipated anew. Routine pianist—even in the routine of the illustrious—Miss Novaes will hardly be for years to come. She is still in the days of ripening.

V

VIOLINISTS

I. "FATHER" AUER

NOW Pugnani taught Viotti; and Viotti taught Rode; and it was the end of the eighteenth century. And Rode taught Böhm; and Böhm taught Joachim; and Joachim taught Auer; and it was the end of the nineteenth century. Then Auer taught Heifetz and it was the beginning of the twentieth and these days.

So runs, like a verse in the Book of the Chronicles and in clearer descent than some which it records, the royal line from 1731 to 1922 that, whatever the accident of individual nationality, has perpetuated the Italian school of violin-playing and faithful to an august standard, has set the making of music, in the finer sense of the words, above the display of skill. Of this illustrious company in our time, Joachim never condescended to the United States; "transcontinental tours" were no institution in his prime; while the America of his imagination was the country and the folk he remembered from the tales of Chateaubriand and Cooper. As surely, had not war and revolution altered the face of Russia, Auer would never have crossed the seas. Pupils from the four corners of the earth flocked to him at Petrograd; he enjoyed life there as it went under the vanished Tsars; his fullest years were his years in Peter's capital. Yet to New York he came in his seventy-third year, and once more the concert-room, from which he had long withdrawn, tempted him. Up and down America had gone his pupils from Mr. Elman and Miss Parlow to Eddy Brown and Jascha Heifetz, spreading directly the fame of their master. Surely American eyes were eager to see, American ears to hear, the violinist who had nurtured such violinists.

Obviously, in the test, Auer contended with the inevitable handicaps of his years. Even so, he escaped many an infirmity that made the playing of his master, Joachim, in the final years at London and Berlin, a painful disillusion. The Russian's ear was still true; his memory played him no tricks; his hand answered to mental control and imaginative prompting; his sense of quality of tone and befitting style with his several pieces was undiminished. Clearly, for example, as he traversed his program, he differentiated a Sonata of Locatelli, which is music of bold pattern-weaving, interesting chiefly for the course and the contours of the melodies and the play of figure within and around them, from a Concerto by Nardini in which tonal beauty and feeling no less than tonal design and progress invite the ear. He was as direct and austere with a stripped sonata out of Händel, as he was graceful and elegant with a serenade and a quick movement transcribed from Haydn. It is possible to object that Auer reduced fragments of Bach to the voice of salon music—yet Johann Sebastian was not above the entertainment of the petty court of Anhalt-Cöthen—but his playing of Vitale's Chaconne, a violinist's test-piece, lacked neither ample and sonorous voice nor large and stately progress.

Such perception and discrimination, instilled and cultivated by master in pupil, stands clear in the playing of Mr. Heifetz, once stood clear in the playing of the younger Elman. Mr. Heifetz's tone owes its unique quality to the mingled sensitiveness and freedom of his bowing, to like play of fingers upon the strings. If in the toll of the years Auer could no longer gain complete freedom, he still kept sensitiveness of hand and ear. To this day, Mr. Elman is pleasurably vivacious when he plays those allegros in the elder music of the violin that are but bright and lively pattern-weaving. His master, at more than twice his age, could summon a like lightness of tone and accent. Who that has heard Mr. Heifetz play the Chaconne of Bach or the Chaconne of Vitale has forgotten the large, expanding, proportioned, contrasted design in which the youth fashions the two musics; how they seem to create themselves under his inciting hand; how strand after strand is spun, set in march, diversified, developed, woven into the texture and the progress of the whole; how a grave and warm directness gives new vitality, new impression to the music? To hear Auer play this same Chaconne of Vitale was to understand that even Heifetz has bettered his instruction only with play of youthful prowess and of innate violinistic instincts that excel in themselves his master's. The model stood clear.

And so forth and so onward with twenty tokens of that teaching by which Auer cultivates the abilities and the impulses of pupils until, upbuilding upon his foundations, they excel, or bid fair to excel, their master. But like the finest and the truest of them, he gave proof of that devotion to the unalloyed voice of the violin and to the unclouded speech of music which is the glory of those Italian traditions and standards. Mr. Heifetz, Mr. Spalding, Mr. Kreisler and a few others have them now in their keeping. From Tartini, Corelli, Pugnani, Viotti they have endured for two centuries and a half through Rode, Joachim and Auer; by the practice and what in time may be the teaching of the violinists now in young or matured prime, they promise to continue into the generation to come. They affirm the obligation of the violinist to set forth his music in the speech of the composer as closely as he may apprehend it, as clearly as he may project it, without thought of distortion of it to himself or of display through it of his own powers. They bid him be musician before he is violinist and so surrender himself to his music. Again they enjoin him to use the violin for neither feat nor trick Paganini-wise, but to draw from it with arm, wrist and fingers, to hear with the finest ear, to direct with the most sensitive control in mind and spirit, the unmatched beauty and expressiveness of voice that it will give back to those so cherishing and guiding it. There is high faith, a noble devotion in those Italian standards, alike with music and with instrument. Not another code for the violin is comparable with them.

II. Kreisler—The Man in the Music

Before Mr. Kreisler's tone, listening becomes a spiritual faculty. No other violinist so melts the listening mind, ear, heart into a common pleasure, a sublimated and suffusing sensuous delight. He keeps his tone like a finely spun thread of beautiful, penetrating, exquisitely modulated sound, never halting, never breaking, never losing either resilience or glamour, a sensitive and subtle speech that quickens in turn the finest sensibilities of those that hear.

Yet so universal is Mr. Kreisler's genius that he is one of the few virtuosi of our day who draws all sorts and conditions of listeners, from the adept and discriminating to the mere seekers of entertainment. Those upon whom Mr. Kreisler, the personality expressing itself through his violin, exercises an endless fascination, sit beside those who find a lasting satisfaction in his finesse as technician, in his insight with the pieces in hand, in his felicities of style. Those who hear only his silken tone, shining with delicate lusters, stand elbow to elbow with those who almost forget the violinist when he carves cameo-like some pattern of ancient music, or glorifies with zest of hand and fancy some trifle from his own or another's pen.

And what an ingratiating and stimulating figure Mr. Kreisler is, in his own right as it were, when he comes upon the stage—this plain man without a trick of manner, without a touch of affectation, without a hint of self-assertion! In his springy stride, which seems to halt only because there is an edge to the stage, speaks his elasticity of spirit; his quiet pose suggests its concentration; his clear glance its poise and its faculty of illumination. He plays and he seems to take no thought of his audience; he is not on view before them to prove by the motions of head and body his response to his music. He does not consult the ceiling; knit or relax his brows, or weave back and forth after the manner of elephants in chains. Unaffectedly he sinks himself in his work; for the time he persuades his audience to hear only the violin, the music and the Kreisler who is content to be their glorifying voice. They said that Paganini's playing was a magic of the devil. Kreisler's has a finer magic —the magic of entire self-subordination. Among violinists, he is as Dr. Muck among conductors, as Mr. Hofmann among pianists, the servant of his music, his instrument and his artistry and so the master of all three.

Mr. Kreisler's programs usually include pieces out of the composers of the seventeenth and eighteenth centuries—from Bach, Mozart and Gluck, from the French miniaturists, Couperin and Cartier, from Pugnani, Corelli and Tartini. Often they are the music of court and salon, slender or ample in form, grave or gay in mood. Obsession as they sometimes seem with him, yet do they disclose many of the finer qualities of his playing, as perhaps no other numbers do. More: he even persuades his hearers to take thought of these pieces apart from violin and violinist. All this music, moreover—and Mr. Kreisler's own trifles with their touches of eighteenth-century melancholy, and even Paganini's masking of technical feats under fanciful or eloquent exercise—exists for its own charm and its own beauty and for such other charm and beauty as the violinist may add to them. Since it is such, Mr. Kreisler's zest for it and perfections in it are easy to understand. Another violinist might match him in knowledge of his instrument, might possess his technique, tone, even his illuminative faculty of imagination. Yet would he lack the fine impulse to the flowering fancy of Gluck's melody; feel not the gentle wistfulness of Couperin; hear no voice of old in the Viennese Caprice; discover no large, free, fertile improvisation in the Italian pieces; and see or hear no patterns dancing upon the air in Bach's Suite. In Kreisler, imagination becomes emotion and when imagination and emotion are so fused and of such effect they are the attributes of genius. For genius—the special election for special work by fore-ordering and fore-equipping fate—is the alembic through which Mr. Kreisler distills tone, and technique, imagination and emotion, violin and music.

III. Heifetz, Newly Ripening

At each hearing of Mr. Heifetz he gives fresh proof of the qualities that have, in so short a time, set him among the illustrious violinists of our day. He has given such voice to the ancient classics of the violin, to Bach's and Vitale's Chaconnes, for example, as the ears of this generation have heard only from Mr. Kreisler. Once more, at his hands, as at Mr. Kreisler's, the violin has become what it really is—especially in distinction above the piano—an aristocratic instrument.

In the bearing of Mr. Heifetz toward his audiences there is also hint of this aristocracy; for unlike one or another violinist of these days, he comes out of no common Russian Jewry, but of an ancient and cultivated Hebrew family, long practicing the arts of music within and without the synagogue. So born and bred, accustomed to public appearance from childhood, his repose upon the stage is both natural and becoming. Even now, when he is plainly in transition from the impulses of youth toward the impulses of manhood, the tension within but tightens the outward calm. The very impassiveness of face and body, resented by some of his hearers, commend him. Because one happens to be by inclination and profession an executive artist of music, must one, therefore, wear one's mind and heart on the sleeve for the gaze of audiences? Enough, and more than enough, in the name of a decent reticence, that the mind and the heart, as Mr. Heifetz's surely do, pervade the playing. Better the concentration and the passion within that guides, consciously or unconsciously, each stroke of the bow, every play of the fingers; better the spiritual intensity sending forth each period of the music as though it were created anew, than all the soulful upturnings of eyes ceilingward and the swayings of body like pump to an oversentimentalized melody.

To be poised before an audience, like Mr. Heifetz, neither courting nor disdaining it, is to hold the artist's powers in firmer, finer leash for the task in hand, for the pleasure to be bestowed. Yet to call this aspect, this demeanor impassive, is not to name it quite accurately, since in the gravity of Mr. Heifetz before his hearers is clear individualizing quality. Whereas Mr. Zimbalist, for example, is impassive, almost negative, to the eye in the concert-room, Mr. Heifetz seems unmistakably intent upon his music, his playing. For the time, they absorb him until, for him, there is naught else in the world. Once embarked upon concerto, sonata, suite, merely miscellaneous piece, he and it —the music, the violinistic means, the medium that he himself has become—are all inextricably fused. Out of him rapt, the breath of genius blows upon an audience.

For no word short of genius may now be advisedly used of the qualities that make Mr. Heifetz in his early twenties one of the few signal violinists of this day. The eye, inevitably, discovers his youth; but not until recently has the ear noted signs of counted and changing years. Even so, the quality of tone little reflects this maturing. It remains the voice of the violin, absolute and unalloyed—not the more or less individualized tone of other illustrious violinists of the hour. As often as not it remains also the perfect voice of the music. Only when the phrases broaden and the accents sharpen, when the lines move more largely and the periods deepen and swell, does the changing Heifetz draw the bow.

He may do what technical feats he will with the ease, the certainty, the brilliance of the flash of a jewel when light catches and penetrates it; but they remain to the essential qualities of his tone what the staccati, the scales, the *mesa di voce* of an ornate singer are to her real mastery of the art of song. Without the extraordinary skill and sensibility of hand and without the equal fineness and susceptibility of ear, he could not do these feats as he does, however much innate instinct and arduous practice might serve him. In those same qualities of hand and ear dwells the secret of a tone, the like of which in intrinsic beauty, in pure and quintessential voice of his instrument only Mr. Kreisler and Mr. Casals may now draw from wood and strings.

More and more, as it seems, this tone tends to take texture and tincture, progress and motion, from a mind and spirit individually stirred. For a time, it was the abstract and absolute perfection of Mr. Heifetz's playing that most possessed his audiences. They heard the voice of the violin conveying unflawed the voice of the music unclouded. No interpreter, as the stock phrase is, stood between hearer and composer, no moodiness in the violinist interposed upon the instrument. Along the stream of tone flowed the piece in hand, while the violinist himself threw no reflection upon this unspecked current, stirred no eddies along its course. With the ripening of Mr. Heifetz from youth to man, inevitable change has come. The impulse has normally entered into him to re-create the given music in his own image, to make the violin speak for himself as well as for the composer. As yet these reactions are somewhat blurred, the will to convey them discoverably groping for the way. Then, for the instant, flaws scratch the younger perfection, the tranquil luminosity of the unquestioning years becomes obscured, the chroniclers write of a time of transition. Through such years of struggle and mastery Mr. Heifetz now goes. Already, however, dart out of them the hours in which he holds the goal and summons the means. Then his playing of Bach, for example, sounds with the breadths, the depths and the heights of ardent re-creation; while shadowed old eighteenth-century masters are of a sudden incandescent again.

IV. Zimbalist Seeking Beauty

Mr. Zimbalist has ripened into maturity in those qualities that made him from the first a notably individual and isolated violinist. He was, when he first came to America, and he is now, the violinist of the abstract and disembodied beauty of the voice of the violin and the music that serves it. In those days his tone had a rare limpidity and softness. It was delicately luminous; it was quite without edge; it had the pure beauty of disembodied sound. It is richer and warmer now; it has gained that penetrating quality which individualizes the violin among other instruments. In the sheer feeling for it that caresses its secrets from it and makes the violinist and the violin each an inseparable complement of the other, Mr. Zimbalist is most like Mr. Heifetz. His deep devotion to the abstract beauty of his instrument and his music isolates his temperament and defines his playing.

Mr. Ysaye's puissant nature magnified pieces and performance; Mr. Kreisler attunes both to the fineness of his spirit; Mr. Elman, unless he curbs himself, plays upon the easier sensibilities of his hearers; Mr. Spalding vibrates between a gravity almost austere and a soft Italian glow. Mr. Heifetz and Mr. Zimbalist make pure distillation of music and instrument. In the younger man went hint of uncanny perfection, whereas Mr. Zimbalist works his clear will upon both. There is not a violinist who seems so negative as Mr. Zimbalist—until he plays. He disdains to cultivate his audience, yet no more would he be deliberately indifferent. Without a trace of self-consciousness he comes, he goes. Always his aloofness is the aloofness of a reticence with self, of a whole-minded absorption in the chosen task.

Sometimes in his miscellaneous pieces at the end of a concert he will include some fashionable piece of the hour—Sarasate's fantasia upon Bizet's "Carmen," for instance. It vies with Liszt's familiar and similar fantasias for piano in epitome of the chosen opera, in vivid suggestion of the illusions of the theater. And Mr. Zimbalist plays it as bravura piece for the violin. Nineteen out of twenty listeners are "programing" and dramatizing it. Yet for him it is as "absolute" and self-contained as though it were Reger's Prestissimo or the sixth variation of Corelli. His mind, hand and spirit know no other way; yet thereby he is rare and precious violinist.

V. Spalding Taking Thought

Our public needed several years to learn that Albert Spalding had become, in his days of study and public performance abroad, an impeccable virtuoso, an understanding musician and an artist with an individuality and style of his own. It chose to mistrust because he had been overzealously heralded on his first appearance here. It may also have doubted because he is American by birth and breeding and therefore without the glamour that often sheds itself upon less well-equipped and less deserving virtuosi of foreign birth and fame.

He has won his present position, then, as he has won all else in his career, by no other virtues than his own assiduity, ambition, standards and self-ripening. So doing, he won deservedly, hearteningly. For several years, it was his way, on each new appearance, to reveal or heighten some signal quality as musician and man. During these years, however, the power of complete revelation, the ability to make the music in hand sound as if it were newly created as he played it, seemed to elude him. Then of a sudden (and not longer than 1916) to his old command of technique and tone, to his old insight and high musicianship, he added the transmitting and transfiguring force which he had hitherto lacked. Now, he plays with an exceeding opulence of tone, as resonant as it is rich, as sensitive as it is full-bodied and songful. This tone on the technical side is born of a very full, fine and ready mastery of the technique of the violin. It is born no less of that musical intelligence by which violinist, pianist or singer hears himself and measures and orders accordingly the quality of his particular voice. It is born, yet again—and for final glory—of that instinct and affection for an instrument that gives it confidence —to follow a not altogether fanciful idea—to speak its secrets into his ears and, through him, to the attending listeners. It is the mark of the artist of the illustrious line—of Mme. Culp, for example, in song; of Mr. Gabrilowitsch, with the piano—to possess this instinctive and affectionate command of his medium.

In more respects than one the playing of ancient music is the criterion of a violinist. The rhythms beat, the phrases expand, the melody takes shape and progress, ornament runs beside it. And lo!

the pattern is woven in a fine ecstasy of assured creation, though the music may have been all in the day's work for busy Bach or diligent Tartini, who did their "job" quite as often as they composed for themselves. But in them was that perpetual fountain and perpetual passion of creation in tones that are the perpetual pleasure and excitement of this elder music—the passion and the plenty that make the formal prescriptions seem the willing servants of the beauty and the power that were in the spirits of these men when they so spoke forth. The imparting violinist must speak as nobly, as abundantly, as passionately as they and then will he transport his hearers into the very thrill and joy of this creation. It is this miracle that Mr. Spalding works.

VI. Thibaud, the Finely Strung

Jacques Thibaud is a patrician among violinists. And so, since a virtuoso's personality will play into his outer semblance, no matter how continent he may be, it is interesting to watch the rare lightness and suppleness and sureness of his bowing and fingering. They seem the outward and visible signs of the sensitive and high-bred spirit, the elastic and certain command within. Whatever the music, Mr. Thibaud's tone in itself is not quite like that of any other violinist. It is not a very fine tone, like Mr. Kreisler's; it is not a very big tone, as Mr. Ysaye's was; it is not the disembodied tone of Mr. Heifetz or Mr. Zimbalist. It is rather a tone of soft and velvety texture, of caressing warmth—a tone that persuades the ear rather than penetrates it; a tone that glows softly with the colors that the violinist sheds upon it. No violinist that plays in these days, not even Mr. Kreisler, plays Bach as does Mr. Thibaud. He opens the music; he weaves and interweaves its many strands; he contrasts, coalesces and colors them. Other violinists may have done as much for Bach's pieces but, most of them, so doing, merely set them forth. Where such end, Mr. Thibaud begins. He gives the music its propulsive force; makes it sound as though it were born of creative passion, almost of creative inspiration.

He excels also with the music of Mozart, the skeleton forms of the early concertos in particular. With them the composer was often his own violinist. If not, according to the custom of those days, he left much to the performing virtuoso, who might be finely strung musician as well. The violin-part—and still more the accompaniment—were no more than hints from the composer. The dexterity of the orchestra would fill out his measures; the violinist, according to his degree, would add skill and taste, discernment, artifice. A first movement with two motives in interplay, "passage-work" for the violinist's plasticity and finesse, songful measures for his sentiment; a slow movement of silken melody, melancholy of mood; a light and glinting finale and the concerto was done—for a Mozart in perpetual flow of music through an easy-going day.

Such a violinist of Mozartian time, skill, imagination, is Mr. Thibaud. His tone glows with soft lusters; it moves in delicate undulations; it insinuates its own beauty and the beauty of the music into ear, mind and fancy. The "passage-work" of a first movement becomes a fine tracery of sound, a veritable embroidery upon the air, spun in tone that catches the lightest inflection of the composer, the slightest impulse of the violinist. A gentle sentiment plays through the songful measures while at every turn Mr. Thibaud gives them that light quiver, that delicate vibration upon air and ear which are life to such music. In this tremor—for it is hardly more—is the secret loveliness of such Mozartian song. Few musicians, singing his songs, playing his piano-pieces or his concertos, divine it. Fewer still impart it. In high degree Mr. Thibaud does both and in penetrating sensation upon his hearers draws from Mozart a hidden and characteristic beauty.

Passing to the final movement, the Rondo, he will make caprice vie with elegance. He will make it no "brilliant finale." Rather he will keep the return of the motives, the rhythmic élan, the flow of the figures, the little in-takes, as it were, of sustained song in light, fanciful, sportive play. Mozart, like the other composers of his day, would give these Rondos the voice, the air, of gay and adept improvisation—the conjurer in tones at final shake of his magic sack. Mr. Thibaud catches the intent, conveys the illusion. Throughout he is not merely faithful to his composer. He divines him. He serves this divination with means free from every technical, every temperamental infirmity. He is wont to pursue an ideal perfection. Often he attains it and the concert-hall, when he does, may know no deeper delight.

VII. Elman, for Better or Worse

Each time that Mr. Elman is heard he seems more and more to stand at the parting of the two roads that a virtuoso of the violin may take. If he chooses, Mr. Elman can definitely take the road that will make him a "popular" violinist, sure of audiences of a sort and more and more disposed to minister unto them. He ministers to them now when he plays with the contortions of his body that have replaced his former "weaving," as though he were in mighty effort to release the emotions surging out of him through his violin. On this score Mr. Elman sorely needs either a sense of poise or a sense of humor. He ministers to such auditors, again, when he seems to squeeze out his instrumental songs as though his violin were a paint tube from which in travail of spirit he was pressing them. He ministers to them, finally, when, in songful or sharply rhythmed transcription, he draws out the song in long reaches of sentimental tone or underscores each beat of the measure. From his beginnings in America, Mr. Elman's temperament has seemed exuberant. At first the outlet of it was the fine fire that he used to bring to Tschaikowsky's concerto, for example. This fire has been less bright of late, and in its stead has come the tendency to exaggeration, and even to showiness. Therein commonness and a kind of popularity lie. In more respects than one this road may tempt Mr. Elman, but it is also a way that by twenty other qualities of his playing he ought not willfully or mistakenly to choose.

He can still "read" the classical sonatas with young sensibilities and enthusiasms. He seems never to suspect that they are classics and that there are traditions in the playing of them. To him, they are only music, full of its own beauty, grace and vitality. Other violinists give it various distinctions; he restores it often to the freshness with which the first listeners may have heard it. Similarly the quality of Mr. Elman's tone seems to point him along the road that the true virtuosi of the violin take to enduring distinction.

Perhaps when a violinist begins as Mr. Elman did as an acclaimed and eloquent prodigy exciting the vague curiosity and the momentary admiration of those that know little and regard even less the glories of the instrument and its music, come such years of opposing tendencies and wavering indecision. The world knows how Mr. Kreisler, who was also a prodigy, emerged out of them along the road that he now follows and to what place as virtuoso, musician and man it has led him. It knows also what fate has overtaken others, who shall be nameless and who have chosen the more tempting way. Not indefinitely will both be open to Mr. Elman, if indeed they still are. Like the rest of us, virtuosi of the violin harden into habits, which are not standards.

VIII. Ysaye and the "Grand Style"

When Mr. Ysaye put by the violin to become orchestral conductor, his choice left an appreciable gap in the public imagination. The expert and the dilettanti may have debated at will and length his qualities and attainments in comparison with the other virtuosi of the bow and string; but in the general mind Mr. Ysaye had become the foremost of living violinists. There was reason for the public so to regard him. He was an imposing figure in the concert-hall. Grandiloquence was his way with music. He was the last of the great violinists to cultivate the "grand style." In the old days when he played his black locks tossed about his forehead and his great body swayed to and fro in the unfolding of a melody, at the climax of advancing progressions.

But Mr. Ysaye, like other of the greatest and the truest artists of the theater and the concert-hall, underwent the spiritualizing process of ripening time. It was as though he had distilled his artistry into the finest, concentrated essence;

stripped himself of all superfluities; as though his personality, his music and his utterance of both had become fused into a single and simplified whole. He may have seemed to do less, since he put aside all personal display for the sake of display, and all musical effect for the purpose of the effect; yet he really accomplished more. As, with the years of richest maturity, he simplified his technical resource and attainment, so also he spiritualized the tone that he produced. The style of his maturity was a style for which he had polished every technical means and in which he practiced every felicity and finesse of exquisitely sure and supple resource. The tone that this technique spun was, in turn, of golden mellowness; it persuaded the ear and warmed the spirit as by some gentle and glamorous magic. It was a ripened, idealized, spiritualized playing of the violin and its music. To the very end of his days as virtuoso, however, Mr. Ysaye could, when the music bade him, summon the violin to a mighty eloquence. He could mingle the fine felicities of his later and maturer years with the tonal sweep and rhythmic fire that made him unique among violinists of living memory. He could still make his great effects of power, when the voice of his violin was as the sound of many voices, when the depths, the breadths, the sweeps and the glows of his tone seemed unmatched and unmatchable. He could transfigure the music he was playing, however commonplace, giving it the voice of his own imagination and his own passion. It is the virtue of the "grand style," the final attribute of it to do so.

IX. Casals, the Unchallenged

Pablo Casals has been much less acclaimed than his established reputation as the most remarkable violoncellist of our time warrants. No country, no capital of music, hears him too often; to America he has come sparingly; usually he shares his recitals; while in the concert-hall he is a pale, an impassive figure. Once set to his work, his playing wholly absorbs him; his bowed countenance remains grave and motionless; he has scarcely a trick of manner; as a physical presence indeed he disappears in piece and performance. His audiences, therefore, do not include those who care more for what a performer seems without than for what he does within.

Before all else, Mr. Casals is ripened and assured master of the technique of the violoncello. He plays it, on the one hand, without the smallest hint of labor or display in the accomplishment of bravura passages, difficult transitions or occult harmonics; and he plays it, on the other, with not a trace of exaggeration or sentimentalizing of its deeper voice and songful quality. His intonation proves alike his flawless ear and his unerring hand. He has attained a delicacy of execution that makes the minutest figuration in the music spring in clear and lace-like tracery from his bow. His reticence, his sensibility, his regard for his tone, measured, luminous and flowing, glamour the give-and-take of any miscellany, however severely chosen, with which composers belittle violoncellists.

At one extreme there is not a hint of grating harshness or of thinness in his tone; at the other there is not a trace of the smear, the blur, the over-pressure upon strings and bow by which many a 'cellist fancies he makes his instrument more expressive. Mr. Casals's bowing and fingering are ideally light, elastic, sensitive and felicitous. He does not command his instrument, he caresses it. He plays not merely by ripened skill, full resource and impeccable ear; but he plays also by an innate instinct and aptitude. He was born for the 'cello as Mr. Kreisler for the violin or de Pachmann for the piano. His flawless delicacy matches the pianist's; his technical sensitiveness and surety match the like qualities in the violinist; and he is dowered, like both these virtuosi, with exquisite sense of the tone that he evokes. That tone, beyond all peradventure, is the ideal voice of the violoncello.

Balzac's personage dreamed of a tone in the human voice that should concentrate the perfect beauty of sound. At moments Mr. Casals so concentrates in his tone the perfect beauty of his instrument. It does not lack body and fullness, yet it is altogether limpid; it does not lack warmth and richness, yet it is never thick and sluggish. It flows with edgeless suavity, yet it undulates to every curve of the music and vibrates to every accent that the composer has laid upon it; heat and light are both in it; and not only sensuous beauty and musical sensibility, but a spiritualized intensity distinguish it. Therein it is individual of Mr. Casals and no other, for what the man is underneath—as Mr. Kreisler likes to say—so in the last and fine analysis his tone must be. It is not merely that Mr. Casals draws from the violoncello a tone that seems the ideal voice of the instrument, he draws from it also a tone that through the music opens the alertly perceiving and serenely apprehending mind, the warm, sensitive and manifold imagination, the pure heights and depths of the finely-touched spirit of Pablo Casals himself. He is remarkable man as well as remarkable musician; he is such a virtuoso of the violoncello as these attributes make him.

VI

CHAMBER-MUSIC

I. The Righteous "Flonzaleys"

TO write chamber-music is to write under hard prescription and for the few; to play chamber-music is to strive for perfection, again in a few appreciating ears. Both are antipodes and antidotes to the passion for the obvious, the mediocre, the democratic, now obsessing some of us in "community singing" and other strenuous exercises en masse. No division of music more needs the hand that discerns as well as helps; none more seldom receives it. Hereabouts, however, it has been well and wisely fostered by the late Edward J. de Coppet, who founded the Flonzaley Quartet, and by Mrs. Elizabeth Shurtleff Coolidge, who for a time maintained the Berkshire Quartet, more recently assembled the Elshuco Trio, and, if report runs accurately, still helps Mr. Letz's string quartet along its way; while altogether unobtrusively she has paid for various series of chamber concerts at universities and made it possible for the London String Quartet to visit the major American cities.

While other string quartets have come—and also gone—at the will of founders and sustainers, at the interest or the indifference of "followings," for nearly twenty years the Flonzaley Quartet has kept place in American concert-halls and paid welcomed visits to European. As the Calvinistic catechism contained "the whole duty of man," so "The Flonzaleys" have embodied, to us, the whole duty of chamber-musicians. As in the beginning Mr. Betti and Mr. Pochon still sit in the seats of the violins and Mr. d'Archambault in the chair of the violoncello. Aftermath of the late war substituted Mr. Bailly for Mr. Ara at the viola, but rare or, maybe, presumptuous was any ear detecting change in the quality of tone or the sensibility of the ensemble. No string quartet can excel unless it enjoy such permanence. It is not enough that the four should practice together in private and play together in public—even ad libitum. Nor yet again that they should consciously strive to unify technique and tone, understanding and response, transmission and illumination. Rather they must enter into that instinctive and reciprocal divination of themselves and their music, their means and ends, which flowers—and by sub-conscious process only—in long, close, affectionate intimacy. The final graces of a string quartet are a spiritual growth, a spiritual assimilation. At work and at leisure, such intimacy, such interplay, have been both the choice and the lot of "The Flonzaleys." They themselves have discerned and willed these essential conditions. Mr. de Coppet, founding the quartet, first provided the means; more recently the support of an enduring public has assured them.

So minded, so circumstanced, the Flonzaley Quartet has pursued perfection and, as nearly as is possible to mortal man practicing one of the arts, has kept close upon her ever-receding heels. The first tone of "The Flonzaleys" was a tone of rare fineness, suppleness, sensibility. It was molded in delicate contours, it yielded to every inflection of the music; it was transparent as the day, yet like the day it caught the light and shadow of sunshine or of cloud; it exhaled the simpler beauty of instrumental song; it made magic of the composer's tracery and arabesques. Behind lay a Latin lucidity and elegance, a plasticity of hand and ear, a felicity of understanding and transmission that were new things in chamber-concerts in America. As few had heard them before, now sounded the quartets of Haydn and Mozart, the sonatas of resurrected composers of the eighteenth century, of

Beethoven in his earlier and middle years. There are those who, a little regretfully, would have these beginnings the halcyon days of the Flonzaley Quartet. Let them be content that this early virtue continues undiminished while to it have been added other and greater glories.

For, though perfection may ever speed her feet before her pursuers, yet wider and wider does she spread her mantle. From the serenities, the melancholies, the gayeties of Mozart, from Haydn pensive, playful or merely at manifold pattern-weaving; from the young Beethoven adding to "the best models" the richness of his invention, the ardor of his spirit, the vigor of his hand and the fecundity of his skill, "The Flonzaleys" were bound to go forward. They went and with every year over broadening fields. In one direction, they achieved the songful flood, the endless ripple and glint and glamour of the quartets of Schubert; the eager intensities, the changeful glow, the shadowed strivings, the radiant fulfillments of the quartets of Schumann. The voices that had undulated to classical continence of line and reticence of inflection, now spoke—and not less eloquently—in the bolder curves, the larger emphases, the inspired irregularities, the passionate freedoms of romantic music.

In another direction, "The Flonzaleys" compassed the racial rhythmic tang, the melody of the soil, the folk-song footfall—and the folk-song repetition—of an occasional Bohemian like Dvoràk, of a semi-occasional and a semi-sophisticated Russian. Expanding yet again and deepening withal, they essayed the relatively austere, abstruse, ruminating and remote music of Brahms. Then, first, in a long and sunny progress, reproach overtook them. "The Flonzaleys" are Latins. Therefore when they give voice to music, they incline to lucidity, precision, to the play of lyric impulse in poetry and fancy, to refinement rather than ruggedness. The reasoned perceptions of the mind will not always curb the instinctive promptings of the spirit, and so, like Mr. Toscanini in Brahms's symphonies, they seemed now and again to subdue and transmute to themselves the manifest matter, manner and will of the composer. Yet a limpid and lyrical Brahms (so far as might be even at the hands of "The Flonzaleys") had timely virtue in a day when too many Americans counted Teutonic "interpretations" among the finalities of music. Like reproach awaited Mr. Betti and his colleagues when they ventured among the later quartets of Beethoven. Plausibly, they groped only where the composer also sought and not always found, pursued light where he had left obscurity—and then made rich amends when they rose to the exaltation of his song or caught the fires of his impassioned energies.

This progress "The Flonzaleys" have crowned with their revelation of the chamber-music of our own particular and fruitful day. The quartets of Debussy and Ravel, for example, were not new to most ears hearing them at their concerts. Yet, there, many a listener perceived as for the first time the pith and point of the harmonic texture, the pungent or the subtle play of the instrumental voices, the rhythmic élan at once sustaining and diversifying the tonal progress, the fertility of device, the iridescent imagery, the poised mood that seemed in those days of discovery to give music both a new sensibility and a new precision. It was as though the finesse and the felicity, the perfect perception and the perfect plasticity of "The Flonzaleys" with Mozart had renewed themselves with Debussy and Ravel; as though such little masters of style with the last years of the eighteenth century had been born anew and as fully panoplied into the first years of the twentieth.

Relatively, however, these quartets were "standard pieces" which "The Flonzaleys" might only enrich and refine. Even Reger had his place, diminished though it now be, before they set him—in specimen—in their repertory. Rather, their pioneering works of conviction and courage have been done with the chamber-music of the so-called ultra-moderns—with the quartet of Schönberg, the quartet and the suite of Bloch, the miscellaneous numbers (as the old phrase went) of Stravinsky. To "The Flonzaleys" it has been no concern how their public might receive these adventures. If it was derisive as with Stravinsky, they were prone to reproach themselves, in warrantless depreciation, rather than composer or audience. If it was receptive as with Schönberg, they rejoiced in the just deserts of the music. If their public heard, stirred and wondering, as with Bloch, sufficient unto the day was the return thereof. Enough that in their judgment all these pieces deserved performance; that they had spared not in the pains of preparation; that they had served the new no less zealously than the old; that they had fulfilled the high obligation of their prestige to the mistrusted music of their own time. Artists' honor, loyalties, self-subordination, may hardly go further. So also have "The Flonzaleys" ministered to the lesser lights of music in their own day. They have found room for Griffes, for Milhaud, for the little known Belgians, for overlooked Parisians. Before long, with their present zest for discovery, they may descry the ascendant Italians, the risen English. As for us Americans, Mr. Loeffler has but to write a chamber-piece to lay it in their hands.

For a decade and more the works of "The Flonzaleys" have thus been the works—Mrs. Coolidge's Berkshire festivals aside—of chamber-music in America. It is quite true that the Kneisel Quartet preceded them, opened the way and smoothed it. The misfortune of the Kneisel Quartet, however, was to decline from merit to mediocrity, to chill a public they had themselves warmed, to leave it eager for the fervors and the felicities of "The Flonzaleys." Slowly Mr. Betti and his companions won their deserts, thrice familiar as their quality now seems; yet no less firmly they have maintained, amplified, advanced it. As many cities as will have them may now take recurring pleasure in them—so long as they do not overtax jealously guarded powers, relax cherished standards, disturb necessary leisures, exhaust zest into routine. "The Flonzaleys" began in artistic righteousness. In the fullness of fame and vogue they have unremittingly maintained it. To do so is not yet common record in the annals of musicians in America.

II. The Zestful Londoners

The London String Quartet came as a revelation to American audiences long accustomed to no other standards than those of "The Flonzaleys." The Londoners were novel; they were also and manifestly different. They struck an emotional fire in their playing while "The Flonzaleys" were content with a warm glow. They sought opulence while the older group seeks, and finds, lucidity, elegance, sensuous contour.

Shrewdly and wisely, withal, Mr. Levey, Mr. Petre, Mr. Warner and Mr. Warwick preferred to come overseas unheralded. Even those whose job it is to scan the reviews of concerts in London newspapers little anticipated their quality. Possibly familiarity had accustomed the British reviewers to the signal virtues of the quartet; whereas in America they fell fresh, clear and warm upon newly listening but hardly unexacting ears. They heard an exceeding warmth of tone, full-bodied, rich of pile and texture, brightly colored and, in moments of ardent expression, charged with deep and glowing beauty. Yet not a delicate modulation, an incidental figure escaped the discerning four as they wove and proportioned the web of the music. When that web parted into strands, they set them in clear tracery; they spun no less the finest gossamers of tone. Only now and then did swift and emphatic measures beguile them—and then for a bare moment—out of euphony into sharpness. At ease they could be as fleet-fingered as the composer bids them in the presto of the second quartet of Beethoven's familiar Opus 59, while their more sparkling gradients of tone ascended or descended, outspreading or curling away. They could be as square-cut and sonorous, too, as Beethoven or any other composer enjoined. Their twentieth-century sense of timbres helped them to individualize voices—perhaps even beyond Beethoven's young imaginings. Above all, to the matings and the partings of the four instruments, to their conversations grave or gay, to single speech, to variations here, to full harmony there, the Londoners brought an air of impulse—the composer's, their own, the audience's even (for so their hearers shared the performance). They apprehended clearly the music in hand; they repaced and shaped it diviningly, with reciprocal sense of pregnant phrase

VII

A DISEUSE

I. YVETTE GUILBERT—THE ARTS EPITOMIZED

IN Yvette Guilbert are epitomized a hundred arts of a hundred players. She is the mistress of a diction that the illustrious of the Comédie itself may not excel in polished perfections or even match in imparting vividness. She is capable to this day of sweeps of pose and of graces of pose that Pavlowa might praise; the play of her tones, in her best years, ranged the long gamut of picture and tale, static moods or released emotions that the pieces on her programs exacted. Even now they are incomparable for such purpose except for the instant when they must be the speech of pure song. At one moment her tongue is bitter with the harsh satire of a mediæval monk or poet, at another it is salty with serio-comic ironies. At a third it speaks the exalted speech of transfiguring and upswelling vision. At a fourth it tells a tale as though it were creating it from sight and sound. At a fifth it is merry with gay prattle, and so onward through a list that might make the thirty-nine articles of a speech perfectly attuned to as many matters.

As various is the play of eyes no less eloquent, of features that seem to etch upon themselves what that tongue speaks, or yet oftener what lies behind its sayings. Prompting and guiding all these means are intelligence and spirit, as acute, fine and many-sided as they are alert and quenchless. Tragedy may deepen both tone and feature, comedy may brighten them, irony often creases them, wit smiles over them, the intuition which is close to genius often enhances them.

A characteristic program of Mme. Guilbert will include a few little pieces of the time of Marie Antoinette—"Bergers and Musettes of the Little Trianon," she calls them. Possibly Marie sang them herself when she and her demoiselles d'honneur dallied beside the temples and the fountains in the groves of the garden. Perhaps an attending courtier with a voice and a knack at elegant song, sang them to her while the company listened, as in Lancret's and Watteau's pictures, in discreet attitudes, with a becoming air of melancholy. Whatever the original circumstances they were prettily artifical ditties that warned an imaginary Phyllis against the inconstancy of shepherd swains, that sang the charms and accomplishments of a "cousinette"; that spoke a young girl's longings "for marriage and the married state." And with such songs Mme. Guilbert can summon the mood and manner, touch artifice with artifice and add grace to grace. Elegant longing and sentimental melancholy, with the faintest spice of pretending, might go no farther.

And then will come pieces of robuster stuff, of franker flavor and more human quality in which it is easy to prefer her. They will narrate stories of the monks whom, from the middle ages on, the tellers of folk tales and the makers of folk verse have not much loved. They would make them churlish and clownish, avaricious and libidinous, knaves and hypocrites unredeemed. Upon such songs Mme. Yvette will lavish all her skill of ironic innuendo. Gayly she keeps company with the particular monk who descended upon the good woman of the house, begged for shelter and warmth, and then for bed and board, and finally for the lady herself. She will mock him to his face; perhaps he had his wicked will; perhaps he failed of it; anyhow the answer is written in the intonations that she gives the deriding little refrain and that make doubt (as it often is) piquancy. Boccaccio might have told the tale with like smiling gusto.

Next perhaps stand songs smacking in their turn as heartily and broadly of the rude tongues, the outspoken impulses, the rough fooleries, the blunt, sordid give-and-take of the peasant folk of the French country-side, as do Maupassant's tales of Normandy farms. To these Mme. Guilbert can summon in her tones not only the two tongues but also the two personages of the dialogued pieces, and whether monk or peasant is the target, diversify the refrains with arch and apt mockery.

At the other extreme Mme. Guilbert can be at will both tender and humble, puissant and opulent. Recall her Mary Magdalen in Oriental splendor of presence and possessions going from door to door, yet in humility. Neither great kings, rich merchants nor even the common hangman had pity or place for her. Yet when she came to Jesus of Nazareth, he repulsed her not, but spoke gentle words of pardon and compassion. Then in Mme. Guilbert's tones is the beauty of the merciful and of the pure in heart that Rostand, with all the resources of the theater to serve him, hardly compassed so fully in like scene of "La Samaritaine." For contrast is Mme. Guilbert's other Mary, the mother of Jesus, who went from tavern to tavern upon the holy night in Bethlehem seeking the shelter that at last a manger gave. Again Mary and Joseph speak in her tones; again the inn-folk make answer; the distant bells chime; and on the expectant stroke of midnight—in the diseuse's deepest tones and intensest gesture, in the outpouring, as it seems, of all the forces of her spirit—comes the acclaiming of the newborn Savior of Men.

VIII

DANCERS

I. The Russians Blending the Arts

RUSSIAN ballets, written, mounted and danced by Russians and Russian operas sung in Russian by Russians were a theatrical fashion and almost a theatrical passion of the twentieth century in Western Europe until the late war shattered habits and dispersed pastimes. Spring after spring, through May and a part of June, Mr. Diaghileff's Russian ballet danced in Paris. Summer after summer from the end of June through July it danced in London. Often a company for opera, completely Russian except in the orchestra, accompanied it for the performance of Russian operas in the original text and in trappings from Moscow and Petrograd. Alike for the ballets and the operas, audiences filled every place in very large theaters at very high prices. A part of these audiences assembled because it was the fashion to see Russian ballets and hear Russian operas. As large a part gathered because in dancing, miming and pictorial aspect the ballets surpassed any known to the contemporary stage, and because the music yielded them new, strange, and very penetrating sensations. In parquet and in gallery, Americans were numerous in these audiences and for several years before the Ballet came to America, they, as eye-and-ear-witnesses, recounted to their countrymen these Russian glories. In turn, the correspondents in Paris and London of American newspapers wrote much about the ballets and operas. The names of Nijinsky and Karsavina, the chief dancers, were repeated many times beyond the Atlantic; and even that of Fokine, producer of nearly all these ballets and inventor of many of them, was not unknown over sea.

In the ordinary course of westward progress, the Russian Ballet, as it was speedily called (as if there were no other in its own country), should have visited the United States long before it did. It tarried elsewhere because whenever such an expedition was proposed it exacted what seemed to American managers impossible terms. Whenever negotiations began Mr. Diaghileff, who had final responsibility and authority over all that it undertook, insisted that his company must dance in America in very large theaters to very large audiences at very high prices, as it had in Europe.

It was accustomed to dance no more than four times a week, it must be engaged in toto; it was hard to convince him that New York, Boston and Chicago could provide orchestras worthy of his dancers.

But the war and its consequences altered many things in Europe—among them, evidently, the mind of Mr. Diaghileff. Accordingly he looked to America with a kindly, even a longing eye; he modified his demands to "suit the times," and agreed readily to the reasonable terms upon which the Russian Ballet made its first American tour. It brought its full forces, with the exception of Karsavina, the chief dancer on the feminine side, less distinguished and less individual than her predecessor, Anna Pavlowa, but none the less a dancer who rises high in the second rank. It failed also to bring Fokine, who has since exemplified here a rare sense of beautiful and significant motion, keen imagination and feeling playing through it, and the pictorial, elastic, illusive and seemingly easy coödination of all the elements in an intricate spectacle. In our day no such imagination as his has worked with the ballet on the actual stage to such resulting beauty. Beyond any individual dancer, he made Mr. Diaghileff's ballet what it was. It did bring Nijinsky, who, whatever his idiosyncrasies and effeminacies, then excelled all the dancers of his sex in imaginative variety, felicitous grace and airy lightness of motion.

Nijinsky and Fokine aside, the salient distinction of the Russian Ballet was—and is—its ensemble—its dancing en masse or in divided and subdivided groups wherein each dancer kept clear individuality, yet was a contributing part to an adroitly ordered but seemingly spontaneous whole. The least of the dancers danced with sense of the mimed drama, of the momentary picture, as well as of rhythmed steps and movements. These ballets, moreover, moved against scenery and were clothed with costumes that were a revelation in color to the American eye. Bakst, unsurpassed master then of the richness and the power of color on the stage, ample and free of design, impressionistic often in artistic procedure, was the author of most of the scenery and costumes. A few of the younger artists of the theater made the rest.

As the austere reviewers of Paris and London affirmed, it is true that the Russian Ballet addressed itself to the imagination and the emotions through the eye rather than through the ear, and that in some of its pieces it subordinated the music to the spectacle. On the other hand, it persuaded the fastidious Debussy and the exacting Strauss to write for it; in its repertory was Ravel's most imaginative and vivid music, the ballet of "Daphnis and Chloë"; and it gave to Stravinsky almost the only outlet for his twin faculties of marvelous orchestral dexterity and of pictorial and characterizing suggestion by interval, chord and rhythm.

What then, were the essential characteristics that differentiated the Russian Ballet, like Pavlowa's before it, from the other dancing we in America had known? That these Russians danced better—the simplest explanation—is one of the most misleading, for the elusive difference does not lie in technique. Certainly their technique was expert; all of them did masterful things with no appearance of effort, and many sorts of masterful things. But technique is no more the source of the highest pleasure in dancing than it is in painting, in music, or any other of the arts. It is a channel of communication; it is the means by which the artistic idea comes from the mind of the creator to the senses of the spectator. The Russians, in fact, have so long since brought their technique of dancing, their command of their bodies, their instinct for balance, for energy without exertion, to the highest point that they have been able to develop an art for which that technique exists—namely, the conveyance of choreographic ideas. Mr. Diaghileff's Russians never escaped from their subjection to ideas—and, moreover, to artistic ideas; ideas, that is, conceived at a high pitch of emotional intelligence.

It was, in fact, not in the technical skill of the dancing, but in the variety and imaginative quality of those ideas that the true individuality of the Russian Ballet stood revealed. Take, for example, the dances from "Prince Igor"—in itself a rather tedious opera, founded on a turgid ballad that was foisted on Russian literature by an eighteenth-century forger and has been allowed to stay there to avoid a scandal. How astutely every means that the theater offers was utilized to produce the desired effect: the menace of the coming cloud of barbarians that is to lie for centuries on the desolate face of Russia (for we are in the camp of the Polovtsians, forerunners of the great invasion); not the blusterings of Tamburlaine the Great, but the quiet vigor, half melancholy, half playful, of a tribe that is itself but a little unit in the swarm. To the eye open the infinite horizons of the steppe, with the line of the burial tumuli stretching away to endless times and places; down the centuries, into Siberia. On the ear sounds the long-drawn, iterant music (Borodin drew his themes from Tartar-Mongol sources). The women crouch, unconscious of themselves, or rise and stretch lazy limbs, and in the end fling themselves carelessly prone when their dance is over. To them succeeds the savage-joyful panther-leaping of the men; the stamping feet and quick nerve-racking beat of the drum; and, more threatening than all, the gamboling of the boys, like kittens unwittingly preparing themselves for the future chase.

Again in Schumann's "Carnaval" was a whole new range of ideas—a series of purely musical ideas, literary or dramatic, it is true, in general scheme—for Schumann himself provided the main verbal notions. Carnaval, Pierrot, Columbine, Eusebius, Florestan—but the inspiration of the details was drawn from music, and certain movements and gestures of the Russian dancers, certain trippings and stridings conveyed humorous fancies which can be conveyed only by music and dancing and which cannot be put into words. This is pure choreography, mimed comment, abstracted from all drama and letters.

On the other hand, as against the expression of a literary-historical idea as in "Prince Igor," or the expression of a half-romantic, half-musical idea as in "Carnaval," the Russians could gain the illusion of remote and detached beauty. In Debussy's "L'Après-midi d'un Faune," for example, there could be no possible illusion of reality; nor yet again the illusion of pure fantasy as in "Les Sylphides." The new intent was a beauty of ancient scene and vesture, of imagined beings as they stirred in Hellenic fancy, and a beauty, likewise, of the sensations—sensations Hellenic perhaps, but quite as much of the place and time of Mallarmé and Debussy, the poet and the composer—that faun and nymphs receive one from another in the scheme of verse, music and mimed episode. Faun and nymphs must be as visualized figments of the stimulated imagination rather than mimes in the flesh; their impulses—for they are not so much as moods—must seem wisps of sensation, flicking the spectator's imagination. Visualized they must be as figures twining about the ancient vase upon which they have been painted, with interlocking and angular arms; or moving their bodies, their draperies, their hands and heads as though they were of a sudden released from the static instant in which the painter had arrested them. Under such intent and necessity there is no dancing "L'Après-Midi," there is no miming it, there is no rhythming it. The players may only accent their gestures and their glances and their movements as the music is accented, and outline their poses to its contours within their steadfast illusion of the figures of vase-painting. So doing, the Russians made this accent a new means of expression that the art of visualization in the theater had hitherto little known or practiced; so doing they visualized in the round and in living beings a beauty of line and color that had hitherto been only of inanimate surfaces; so doing they enriched the theater with a strange and rarefied art that it knew not in its perfection until the day when "L'Après-Midi" was set upon the stage. The Russians further enriched it, and in other ways, with Debussy's "Jeux" and Stravinsky's "Sacré de Printemps" but Mr. Diaghileff did not dare risk them upon a public like ours, little schooled in the elements—to say nothing of the sophistications—of the mimetic arts.

"Of pure mimesis—the imitation of actual material movements—there was but little in the Russian Ballet. Still less was there of convention, that mysterious language of gestures with which ballet-masters are wont to darken the mind of the spectator. Neither did it seek to entertain us by the mere portrayal of such simple matters as love, invitation, refusal, indignation and forgiveness. To make it worthy of its purpose there must be some individuality in the emotions, which gives it a new significance. Pavlowa, for instance, does not so much imitate the movement of a butterfly as the emotional quality of a butterfly-flight, the sense raised in our minds by watching it; and then it is not an ordinary butterfly, but a Grimm butterfly, a dream butterfly, a butterfly multiplied many times by itself, raised as it were to the Pavlowa-th power.

"When for a moment the Russians are confined to mere imitation—the representation, for instance, of the joy of youth—they catch newly expressive gestures, such as that wholly childlike, bold swinging of the arms, as if they were pinned on at the shoulders. In all ballet-dancing there is a dim attempt to represent the spiritual, the fantastical, by means of the material; the tiptoeing and the lifting-up of the women is a suggestion of the ethereal; but the perfect ease and grace of the Russians enables them to carry this to a far higher point than any others have done, so that in their suggestion of things flying, things swimming, things poised, or things blown in the wind, the sense of the material passes away altogether.

"The art of the older ballet turned its back on life and on all the other arts and shut itself up in a narrow circle of tradition. According to the old method of producing a ballet, the ballet-master composed his dances by combining certain well-established movements and poses, and for his mimetic scenes he used a conventional system of gesticulation, and endeavored by gestures of the dancers' hands according to established rules to convey the plot of the ballet to the spectator. Not to form combinations of ready-made and established dance-steps, but to create in each case a new form corresponding to the subject, the most expressive form possible for the representation of the period, the character and the idea represented—that was and is the first rule of the Russians under Diaghileff.

"The second rule is that dancing and mimetic gesture have no meaning in a ballet unless they serve as an expression of its dramatic action, and they must not be used as a mere divertissement or entertainment, having no connection with the scheme of the whole ballet. The third rule is that the new ballet admits the use of conventional gesture only where it is required by the style of the ballet, and in all other cases endeavors to replace gestures of the hands by mimesis of the whole body. Man can be and should be expressive from head to foot.

"The fourth rule is the expressiveness of groups and of ensemble dancing. In the older ballet the dancers were ranged in groups only for the purpose of ornament, and the ballet-master was not concerned with the expression of any sentiment in groups of characters or in ensemble dances. The new ballet, on the other hand, in developing the principle of expressiveness, advances from the expressiveness of the face to the expressiveness of the whole body, and from the expressiveness of the individual body to the expressiveness of a group of bodies and the expressiveness of the combined dancing of a crowd.

"The fifth rule is the alliance of dancing with other arts. The new ballet, refusing to be the slave either of music or of scenic decoration, and recognizing the alliance of the arts only on the condition of complete equality, allows perfect freedom both to the scenic artist and to the musician. In contradistinction to the older ballet it does not demand 'ballet music' of the composer as an accompaniment to dancing; it accepts music of every kind, provided only that it is good and expressive. It does not demand of the scenic artist that he should array the ballerine in short skirts and pink slippers. It does not impose any specific 'ballet' conditions on the composer or the decorative artist, but gives complete liberty to their creative powers." *

* From the *London Times* passim.

II. The Poetry of Pavlowa

It was the Diaghileff Ballet that first brought Pavlowa to Western Europe from the Russia where she was high-placed ballerina in imperial opera houses. A few years later she assembled a company, including Michael Mordkin, and began to produce ballets in her own right. Under these circumstances she gave to America the first important glimpse of the beauties of the Russian ballet and its coördinating arts. She has since become ceaseless wanderer on the face of the globe, carrying with her the beauty of the dance as it has not manifested itself in any one person in our day.

Year after year Pavlowa has revealed to us the range of her resources, the diversity of her accomplishment, technical and pictorial, imaginative and emotional. She has run the whole gamut of technical means and technical achievement. It is not merely that Pavlowa accomplishes every feat of technical virtuosity with exceeding plasticity, with exceeding sureness, with an air, almost, of simplicity in the doing of the intricate and of spontaneity in the compassing of the involved. It is rather that Pavlowa gives to these feats of high technique a beauty of line in swift and rhythmed motion that makes them seem to spring out of the imagination in themselves, like the emotion of absolute music. She falls into a pose; the technician can derive from it on the instant one or the other classic "position"; yet the eye sees first and feels longest the exquisite beauty of line. The impression is as though fluid motion were arrested for an instant to expand in static beauty, as the running brook halts for a moment to make a sunlit pool. Or the impression and emotion are of the winged lightness of the movement, the blending of each one of its parts into a single lovely flash. Such technique has impalpability; it is like air in motion; it is as fluid as water; as swift as fire. Here is the beauty of motion in its distilled essence, as indefinable by word as the absolute distilled beauty of music, but as recognizable and real—more real even than reality.

The nearest approximation to the classic ballet, as of old it went in the capitals of Central and Eastern Europe, came to the present generation of our stage in Pavlowa's ballet-pantomime of "The Sleeping Beauty." There was the Russian Ballet of Diaghileff and Nijinsky; there is, or was, the Russian Ballet of the state theaters in Petrograd and Moscow. The one was the handiwork of innovators, individualists, seceders, designed less for a Russian than a cosmopolitan audience. It mimed quite as often as it danced. The other exemplifies, preserves and enriches the tradition that began when the first French and Italian dancing masters were summoned from the West to bring their method with them. It exalts the formalism and the virtuosity of the dance.

"The Sleeping Beauty" is such a ballet. Tschaikowsky finished the music in the prime of his powers, and, as his friends recall, was better satisfied with it than with anything he had done for the theater. As the tradition prescribed he wrote it to an appointed scenario, carefully divided and subdivided into the number of measures the omnipotent ballet-master chose to allot to each dance and each mimed episode. It does not lack the stately graces that become a formal and somewhat rococo ballet; it has many a moment of lyric warmth or rhythmic glow; it is like a mirror for the varied reflections of story and action.

The fable is the familiar folk-tale of the lovely

young princess, for whose hand many noble youths sued, who was protected by the good fairy, yet was cast into deep sleep in the forest by malign magic and there lay until the bravest and the most devoted of her suitors wakened her and restored her to human love and happiness. A pale, transparent, even childlike fable, as most fables of Russian classic ballets are; but one that the dullest may not misunderstand, that is rich in opportunities for the dancers and in invitation to the decorators. And when Bakst set to the designing of the backgrounds and costumes, he took thought of the period in which Perrault wrote his fairy tales and of the great rooms and formal gardens in which his readers conned them. The sobriety and the formalism of the backgrounds, the unemphasized line and the subdued color were new notes in Bakst's work as America had hitherto known him. Yet it kept its familiar virtues of assimilation of the chosen style, of assiduous harmony with the matter, manner and characteristic suggestion of the appointed ballet. As it conventionalizes the dance, so he conventionalized the decoration. In contrast not a few of the costumes were of truly Bakstian splendor that seemed yet more splendid against the relatively neutral backgrounds.

And according to the prescriptions of the classic ballet, Pavlowa herself danced in the traditional dresses, variously colored, of a prima ballerina—billowing skirt, light bodice and silken fleshings, nearly invisible. Her beauty was the beauty of her own dark features, of her darting arms and gossamer fingers, of her winged feet, of her whole slender, sinewy, alert and intent body. Her artistry was the artistry in which she had been schooled and become perfect in the days of her youth in Russia's imperial theaters. It shone through all the technical feats that the ballet exacted, shone through the glamour of young serenity and surprise, wonder and eagerness, happiness and affection with which she invested them as became a personage who was a fairy-book princess before she was past mistress of the adagios and variations, the posings and flittings of the classic dance. Her own spirit added yet another mantle. Once more she was a creature of light and air who made a transcendent virtuosity, a flawless elegance, a perfect sense of style like wreathing vapors upon the watching eyes and the quickened imagination.

Yet Pavlowa's artistry can be as contemporary as it can be classic. Mlle. Genée herself was not better grounded in all the technical aptitudes of the old classical ballet, but Pavlowa prefers to use them as the instruments of her modernized imagination. Similarly in the decoration of the many stages upon which she dances, she follows the ways of the scenic past when they suit the music and the ballet that she has in hand. But she turns much more eagerly—if she is minded not to be careless—to the methods and the fashions of the present when they bid fair to heighten the illusion that she seeks. With "The Sleeping Beauty," with "The Magic Flute," or with her terpsichorean transcription of Weber's "Invitation to the Dance" she is content with backgrounds of the traditional sort. Passing to her newer "divertissements"; to a highly imaginative ballet of the present, like her version of Liszt's "Preludes"; like her "Orientale"—made from a patchwork of the music of Serov, Musorgsky and Rimsky-Korsakov—she sets around them decorations in the more modern fashion.

"Orientale," like its forerunner, "Thamar," was born of Russia and of the East and of a time that liked fierce passions, high colorings, vivid shapes, and sharp-set music in the theater and liked them the better when they came with barbaric tang.

Instead of a neutral setting, the play of Bakst's hot, broad color over a close-walled Oriental chamber, remote, solitary, perfume-laden, voluptuous in its every suggestion. Instead of merely incidental dresses, costumes that were part and parcel of this play of color and implication. Instead of conventionalized music, music out of the Russians that was as highly colored as the settings, that ran to sharp, wild rhythms, that bore passion and whipped it. Instead of the play of pretty sentiment and light humor, the enchantress waiting for her passing prey, devoured with desire for it, pursuing it with fierce and sensual temptation, almost possessing it, and indomitable still when it slips from her—a mimodrama with passion and fate at odds within it; a mimodrama in which every means was shaped to the stark and graphic end.

Bakst carried the eye and the imagination into the enchantress's chamber. Her women danced there in the languor of the Orient. Her serpent-like priest wrought his incantations over his perfumed jar. And she lay and watched and in imagination devoured the object of her desire. Chance brought him—the younger warrior—to her door. Her soldiers led him within. Upon him she plied all the fierceness of her fascination. Her women danced and now less in languor than in frenzy; her magician wrought his spells; her soldiers in rude dances kindled his native wildness. She herself sprang to lead all this rout. The fire of her passion almost caught him into it to consume him. His talisman saved him. Baffled but still waiting indomitable, she returned to her couch and her vision of new prey. Upon the room settled again the heavy stillness, the fateful solitude.

Pavlowa mimed and danced the enchantress. At first and as it seemed for long, she had only to visualize in the upturned face and the outstretched body the woman waiting tigress-like for her prey, and preying upon herself in the fierceness of her anticipation. Here was Pavlowa's mastery of sustained and static projection not merely of a vivid being but of the fires that smoldered within it. The sight of the young warrior was like the outward flare of them in the wind of the passion. Perhaps, when she set to the dancing and the miming of the enchantress, tempting and almost possessing, she used too often the sharp angular gesture and movement which were becoming an idiosyncrasy of the newer Russian dancing. Yet when she so used it, she plied it with clear purpose and not as the seeming mannerism that Nijinsky so ardently cultivated.

This gesture and this motion were as stark and fierce, as hard and burning as the passion behind. By that passion she would master and devour its object. She did not caress; she commanded. Power was in the miming and savagery in the dance. Then came the climax when the hand is almost upon the prey, and fierce anticipation played out of her graphic glance and her dancing body. Then the moment of fierce bewilderment when the warrior baffles her. Finally, the slow sinking, with the very voice and line of the music, into the waiting, indomitable and devouring. Miming of such imagination and intensity, so stark, so elemental, is revelation of the other Pavlowa—of the actress of passion and power, mate and foil to the wraith, the white flame, of the dance.

III. Manifold Nijinsky

Like Pavlowa, Nijinsky was no contented technician of the dance, superlatively as he could summon the older virtuosity in such pieces in the Russian Ballet's repertory as "The Enchanted Princess" or, in a measure, the quasi-idyllic "Spectre de la Rose." He was schooled in it for nine years, as is every Russian dancer; he practiced it for years afterward in the imperial theaters before a public more expert and insistent with these technical felicities than any other in the world. He still made use of them in mimed impersonation and graphic suggestion remote indeed from the ends for which the older French and Italian ballet-masters designed them.

They conceived the art of the dance as self-contained, self-sufficient, absolute, reward enough in its own agilities, graces, subtleties for those that practiced and those that watched and applauded it. Obviously it asked little of the mind; it gave as little room for any play of the spirit. Yet for the dancer and the mime of these later and newer days who would ply his intellect and set free his fancy and feeling in all that he undertakes, this old virtuosity provides often the apt and ready means—a shading here, a happy stroke there, a luminous point upon an implication that might otherwise be dark, a persuasive suavity that ingratiates and kindly disposes the spectator. The alertness, the patience, the dexterity, the endless quest for exactitude of the elder virtuosity have their uses in the new freedoms. In itself it may be no more than a relatively paltry goal; yet without it the dancer and the mime of these days lacks his tested tools.

Nijinsky often talked in his day, as few dancers can talk, about the art of the dance. Lucidly and with a gentle confidence, he was ready to link the present with the future. He recalled the repertory of the Russian Ballet as it then was: on the one side the pieces that exemplify the dance, —"The Sylphs," "The Enchanted Princess," "The Phantom of the Rose," "Butterflies," "Carnaval" —ballets of atmospheric and poetic suggestion as well as of the skill that they exact: on the other side the mimodramas—"Cleopatra," "Schéhérazade," "Thamar," seeking illusion by acting that should be only the more graphic because it is wordless and using the dance not only as decoration, but also as characterization and narrative. It was possible for him, for Fokine, for the ballet, to continue to multiply either species, deriving a "Butterflies" from a "Carnaval," for example, making the dance serve new fancies, transfiguring as in "Armida's Pavilion" that upon which it had exercised itself of old. Similarly mimodrama could go on with mimodrama—of agonized passion, of Oriental scene. But the outcome would be—to make a kind of paradox—a monotony diversified within itself, content with pretty terpsichorean fantasias or with mimed and excited action. Stravinsky's "Fire-Bird" did little more than blend these fantasias of the dance with quasi-dramatic fable out of old folk-lore. Even "Petrushka" widened the field only by the setting of a fantastic and ironic tale within the busy and realistic action of the booth and the fair.

Yet in "Petrushka," in his view, was the germ of the idea that first persuaded and finally conquered him. Stravinsky and Benois bid the spectators look into the half-human puppet's piteous little soul. He is more interesting, more touching for what he is than for what he does. The interest and the illusion of the fantasias were dynamic, upspringing from the grace, the charm, the beauty of motion. The interest and the illusion of the mimodramas sprang from visualized and intensified action. But the appeal of Petrushka, the puppet, was, to a degree, in what he half-humanly was, in his reactions to his fantastic fortunes. He touched his audience by what it felt about him rather than by what it merely saw him do. Why not, then, go forward to a ballet that should depend much more upon this static suggestion, a ballet that should not be full of dynamic emphasis, a ballet almost—to put an extreme case—without movement?

In "The Afternoon of a Faun," Nijinsky first worked out his idea of a ballet that should be intrinsically static, impersonal, so to say; of spiritualized atmosphere and illusion, of reticent means and of means newly devised or employed. Studious always of pictures and sculptures, the old Greek bas-reliefs suggested the simplicity, the directness, the economy, even the rigidity of line in pose and gesture that he sought. From the actors on the stage of the spoken word, when to their abilities, they add intuition, inspiration and what in short is called genius, emanate, though they speak not and stir not, the sensations, the emotions, the traits of the personage that they are assuming in the circumstances of the play. May not a dancer and mime of the speechless theater so receive, intensify and transmit, so bear to his audience the sensations and the illusions implicit in Debussy's music and Mallarmé's verses? May not he and others besides, into whom he has infused his intent, weave out of pose and gesture and graphic impression, from within outward, an atmosphere like that which Debussy weaves in tones?

So Nijinsky designed and accomplished his version of "The Afternoon of a Faun." So he went forward to Debussy's "Jeux," to Stravinsky's "Sacré de Printemps," neither of which has been seen in America. In "Jeux," he sought to simplify and spiritualize light fancy until the audience should forget that it was looking upon youth that might be on their way to or from tennis, yesterday, to-day, to-morrow, should feel only the play of ever-renewed young moods, caprice, pastime, and coquetry. He pursued a distilled illusion, he used as distilled and concentrated means. So far as he could accomplish his end, the piece—half-mimed, half-danced and sometimes merely a still projection—characterized. In "Le Sacré de Printemps"—spring rites of a primitive and pagan

Russia—he returned to static suggestion, to rigid, sparing but always clearly rhythmed pose, gesture, movement, to this intensified projection by subtler and keener means than action, of the beliefs, the emotions, the ceremonies of primitive folk and faith. Already he had persuaded Stravinsky to his experiments and they worked upon "Le Sacré" in a common courage and loyalty. Then for a year or two he paused for the nursing of new ideas, for the shaping of new designs, for the fresh opportunity. It came with "Till Eulenspiegel," in the graphic concentration of a place, a time, a folk, their moods and their manners, in hint withal at social philosophy. The stage of the mime may thus match, may outdo, Nijinsky believed, the austerer stage of the spoken word.

Who shall say that he did not succeed? For in his definition of Till, he surely fulfilled his own faith in the characterizing arts of the dancer and the mime. In the prank upon the bread-basket went the sportive Till—yet with a more serious intent or two underneath—and the litheness, the swiftness of his rhythmed pillaging had the beauty of the dance. When he mocked the pious pretence of the monks this Till grimaced with his foot, with his whole body. When he pretended to woo the rich and high-placed dames he wove the arabesques of the dance, yet in and through them was the derisive courtier. When he made a mock of pedantic learning he put a kind of counterpoint into his miming.

Then came the Till, all the mantles of disguise thrown aside, who danced in the long swift lines, the great arcs about the square, in the elation of his power and victory, in the happiness of a free spirit. Out of the face, the arms, the whole being of this Till spoke the jest that was more than half earnest when the rabble lifted him to deserved kingship. The miming of Till before the inquisitors was more within the ordinary scope of mimodrama with the twinges and twitches of dread in exact accord with the checked and tremulous leaps of Strauss's music. Then, resurrection and glorification with the outshining from Till of that inner illumination which Nijinsky believed the mime no less than the actor could compass—the triumph of an idea and a temperament in perpetual symbol, the "apotheosis" of the ancient ballet made a thing of simplicity, significance and beauty. In practice no less than in faith Nijinsky did not flag. Newer dancers now carry on these faiths and these practices.

V. Genée's Cool Charm

Adeline Genée was to the very day of her retirement the dancer, par excellence, for cool and cultivated spirits. To the end she kept her hold upon the public that liked her devotion to the classic ballet and that was ever a little dubious over the newer and franker dancing of Isadora Duncan with her train of imitators, and of the passionate and thrilling Russians. Miss Duncan and her progeny danced in a fashion of their own that has widened the expressive scope and vividness of the dance, mated it to new rhythms and new music, subdued its virtuosity and increased its humanity. When the Russians danced, it was with the strange and exotic savor, the mingling of simplicity and sophistication, the passion and the mystery—to us of the Western World—that are in most of the applied arts of the Slav. Alone among the dancers of the first rank that we in America have known, Genée perpetuated the traditions of the classic school—of the dancing that descended from the eighteenth century into the nineteenth, that flowered in the golden years of Taglioni and Ellsler, Grisi and Cerito; fell away into the sterile and finical virtuosity that long flourished on the stages of Paris, Rome and Petrograd; only to rise reincarnated for us of America and England in Genée.

By chance or design—much more probably the latter—she emphasized this descent and heightened this similitude by her choice of pieces. In one she danced and mimed as La Camargo, the illustrious dancer of the Paris of Louis XV, who widened the technical range of the ballet and who, beyond all her sisters of the eighteenth century, clothed her dancing in her own traits and spirit. In another, Genée danced in the ballet of the nuns' ghostly temptations from Meyerbeer's opera, "Robert the Devil." It was a ballet of the thirties and the forties, a "real French ballet" in white tulle skirts and fleshings, as our grandparents would have called it. In such ballets did the dancers of the golden age move. Between whiles, too, Genée disported herself, with her own adept faculty as a comédienne, in light interludes, in fanciful or humorous dances of character.

For those that know and care for the classic technique of the dance and for those that only half suspect, out of quickened feeling, its exactions and felicities, Genée's dancing in the ballet from "Robert" was high, rare pleasure. She accomplished in it nearly every possible feat of virtuosity in a flawless perfection that seemed to rise with the difficulty of the achievement. Her light bounds, her graceful swirls, her rhythmed steps about the stage seemed aërial and bodiless. Her pirouettes were little rhapsodies in technique. Her poses flowed into beauty and grace of line that suggested no effort, that bore not a trace of stiffness. Artifice they were, but spontaneous and beautiful artifice. The subtler attributes and graces of the old dancing shone in her—in the varied poise of her head and shoulders, in the management of her hands, in the keeping of her body in flowing or arrested arabesque. She accomplished all these things with an ease, a sureness, an elegance, a completeness that were style in itself in conscious but unobtruded perfection. Then entered the personality of the dancer to glamour this dancing, in the narrow sense of the word, with beauty and with charm. Meyerbeer's ballet in spite of its elaborate program of temptations expresses nothing to the imaginations of the present but the beauty with which the dancer may clothe it. Dancing in it, nowadays, is "absolute" dancing existing for its own sake and making its appeal in its own right in the fashion of "absolute" music. Since there is no passion or mystery in the music or the imaginings behind, it was at one with Genée's own spirit. She sought the "absolute" and abstract quality of the dance—the body weaving beautiful patterns upon the air, then animating and illuminating them with the glow and the charm of the spirit behind. Of such disembodied beauty was her dancing in "Robert."

The music of "La Camargo" was adapted from eighteenth century sources by Miss Dora Bright. The ballet was set on the stage in a boudoir wherein Boucher's fat and rosy nymphs looked down from the walls. It was diversified by entrances of Louis XV himself, a distressed mother, a half-grateful and a half-anxious soldier. It bade Genée mime as well as dance. She was La Camargo, momentarily melancholy and introspective, while over this disillusion she threw the wistful charm of face and motion which was the counterpart of merriment in the dancer's temperament. She had occasion also to make La Camargo arch, playful, merry, even with the great king who came to see her dance and who was fain to walk a smiling gavotte with her. As it happened, too, the distressed mother and the anxious soldier were no other than friends and companions of La Camargo's village youth, and so Genée could bubble with surprised pleasure at sight of them once more and play at being a peasant girl again.

Genée mimed with many of the conventional signs of the classic pantomime; but she softened and refined them with her individual charm, made her face the clear mirror of what they would reflect, and kept them flowing with an elegant and airy lightness. She could not mime deep and passionate moods, but she could fill surfaces with beautiful light and shade. She danced, too, as La Camargo, in the full flowing skirt and the high bodice that dancers wore in those days, danced in the very entrechats—the crossings of the feet in air—that Camargo herself invented, and in many another fashion that the eighteenth century may or may not have known. Over this dancing she wove the wonted beauty and charm that were in all she did; while costume, surroundings, the little tale, and the pleasant illusion of the eighteenth century touched both with elegance, with fragrance.

V. Isolated Isadora

The charm of Isadora Duncan's dancing in her best days was its exquisite innocence, its exquisite lightness and its exquisite plasticity. Some there were who called it the dancing of the future—which, of course, was pure conjecture. Her advertisements in turn called her dances "a revival of Greek—or was it classic?—art." That designation was no less conjectural. If the archæologists may be trusted, scanty indeed are the accounts of Hellenic dancing, or even allusions to it, that have come down to us.

Whereas Geneé idealized the conventions of the ballet, Miss Duncan in her turn—or Isadora as Europe still prefers to call her—had invented a method of dancing that was and is all her own; that gives oftenest the impression of abstract and remote beauty; and that depends unusually little, little upon the personal charm of the dancer. Whether Isadora ever studied the classical technique of the ballet is not easy to learn. It was her way to wrap all her beginnings in mystery.

At the least, in the nineties, when she was one of the chorus girls of Daly's Theatre, she must have learned something of the ways of ordinary stage dancing. Doubtless those beginnings trained her muscles to supple obedience, doubtless they gave her something of the skill she had in her prime to hide all mechanism; and most surely they taught her much to avoid. There was not a trace of convention in her dancing. She had plainly gone to other models—to Greek and Roman marbles and vases, to Roman wall-paintings, and to the pictures of the more primitive Italian painters. As plainly she studied the rhythmic movements of natural objects, of children, and of untutored folk in unfettered dance. Her dancing seemed less a return to the conjectures of what Greek dancing may have been than a return to nature itself; to dancing as beautiful, rhythmic and expressive motion in all its purity and abstraction. Out of her own imagination, out of her own intuitions and aptitude, she made her own methods, fashioned her own ends and set her own standards. The suggestions from without she wove within.

This dancing was truly all her own: yet as truly it was little dependent on her own personality. Certainly she lacked physical and sensuous beauty either of face or form. She gave no sense of individual distinction. She had no "troubling" semblances, as the French adjective goes. There she was—a woman past her first youth, dark of hair and eye, thin of feature, slight of body, neither short nor tall—in fine, without physical significance of any kind. Yet clearly in her was the spirit that subdues all things to itself. She was interesting, she was unique, not for what she was (which was half the secret of Genée's charm) but for what she did. Moreover, in her dances, all sense of the dancer herself as so much corporeal flesh and blood, vanished. She had become beautiful and expressive and disembodied motion. The nearest and clearest analogy is that of the dancing figures with which the Romans adorned their walls. Isadora seemed as one of these that some magic had set free and that danced upon the air. She was as bodiless as they; she moved with the same infinite lightness; she repeated them in endless variations of their beauty. She was no more tangible than they and she was quite as lovely. The painters and the sculptors of Greece and Rome seized their dancers in a moment of arrested motion, because they could do no more within their arts. Isadora seemed to set that motion free.

Miss Duncan's dancing was graphic of beautiful, sensitive and idealized movement. It was graphic no less of idealized, abstract moods and emotions. It was loveliest of all, for example, when it would express awakening, stirring, mounting joy, when it would attain to a pure and idealized elation. It was graphic, in turn, in its expression of innocence; never was dancing less sensual. It was graphic, too, of moods of wistful longing and wistful tenderness. It had even a passion of its own, a clear soft passion that sought its own ideal of beautiful disclosure. But it was not passionate dancing in the ordinary sense of the word. Take, for example, Miss Duncan's dances to music out of Gluck's "Orpheus." The suggestion of the blessed spirits of the Elysian Fields lay exactly within the range and quality of her artistry and imagination. Then indeed was she a figure of ideal beauty, of truly poetic illusion, of exquisite purity of motion and mood. She had also to suggest Orpheus, distraught at the loss of Eurydice, torn alike with apprehension and anticipation as he makes his way to the underworld. She did indeed imply all this, but remotely, statuesquely, a little coldly. The play of body and face and arms lacked the intensity that we moderns almost unconsciously associate with such passionate grief. No one knows, no one cares whether the miming of the Greeks and Romans suggested such emotions reticently—as reticently as did Miss Duncan—whether they made them less, and not more, human. (Certainly the account of the miming in Anatole France's novel of pagan Alexandria implies no such reticence.) Rather the essential matter is that a dancer here and now should implant Orpheus's grief vividly in us who watch her. At such moments Miss Duncan's lack of passion or suppression of passion, in the ordinary sense of the word, partially defeated her. Recall her programs and they avoided almost always the expression of vehement and consuming passion. Joyous and virginal, she illuded the spectator. Before her, doomed and woe-stricken, he doubted.

In a word, Miss Duncan was the dancer rather than the mime. The mime, as ancient dancing and even modern ballet employs the word, dances to suggest specific emotions, a specific mood, even a specific character. Miss Allan's much debated "Vision of Salome" was not dancing in the strict sense of the term, but miming. She sought to suggest, she did suggest, the Princess of Judæa and the particular episode of the execution of the Baptist. So Thaïs in the episode that Anatole France describes imparts the particular personage of Greek and Trojan legend. When Miss Duncan mimed—in the tale of Pan and Echo, for instance, or the fable of Narcissus, or the passion of Orpheus —it was beautiful miming in loveliness of pose, in grace of movement, in exquisiteness of sugges-tion. It visualized; but it visualized a little tamely, a little in flat tints. The spectator looked upon a picture of Narcissus, a vision of Pan and Echo, as Botticelli or some other primitive Italian painter might have imagined them. There was little sense of the emotions of the youth or the nymphs. They lacked intensity. They were not characterized but pictured. The reason was not far to seek. Luminous as the motions of Miss Duncan's dancing could be; though she could make her arms as beautiful and significant as a line of poetry, her face had scant range of vivid expres-sion. The spectator could read little there but Isadora's absorption in her task, Isadora's smiling joy of it, or at most some generalized emotion. Now one may not mime without very clear and adroit play of feature, and it was on this side of pantomime that Miss Duncan had obvious limita-tions.

Miss Duncan's dancing, because it was so self-contained, so abstract, was more akin to music than to any other of the arts. She liked to dance to a symphony of Beethoven or to fragments of opera by Gluck, or to sober airs of Rameau and other composers of the classic eighteenth century. Yet the sensations the spectator received from her dances were often curiously like those that spring from a symphony of Mozart. The long, flowing line of the music and the dance, ever springing and curving out of itself, were as one. The endless undulation of Miss Duncan's dancing was as the endless undulation of Mozart's music. Each had its points of repose when the dance or the music seemed to crystallize for the instant and then flow onward again. Each had its light, clear beauty, each its grace and ornament. Each, too, sought felicity of design, economy of means. Miss Duncan's dancing was only the development and the variation of certain motions and certain poses; she worked from them, she modulated them, she individualized them as a mistress of the ballet works and imagines and invents from the classic "positions." Mozart in like spirit was economical, inventive, imaginative with his music. Out of little he wove much—and to beauty. Again, there was often a suggestion of joy in Miss Duncan's dances that was strangely like that of Mozart's music, and that similarly beguiled and stirred those who saw or heard. Each had the same chastity of form, mood and impression. On occasion Miss Duncan believed she danced to Beethoven. Almost always she was dancing to Mozart.

THE END